2019 IGE Distinguished Lecture Forum

인공지능(AI)이 만드는 경제·사회의 미래

초판 1쇄 발행 2019년 12월 27일

펴낸이 전광우
지 원 조수영
디자인 김정진
인 쇄 한진기획인쇄

펴낸곳 세계경제연구원
전 화 02-551-3334~8
팩 스 02-551-3339
등 록 서울시 강남구 영동대로 511
ISBN 979-11-6177-014-7

*이 책은 저작권법에 따라 보호받는 저작물이므로 무단 전재와 복제를 금합니다.
*잘못된 책은 구입하신 서점에서 바꾸어 드립니다.

2019 IGE Distinguished Lecture Forum

인공지능(AI)이 만드는 경제·사회의 미래
Jerome C. Glenn

미·중, 한·일 무역분쟁과 세계 무역체제의 미래
Jeffrey J. Schott

인공지능(AI)이 만드는 경제·사회의 미래

Artificial Intelligence (AI) and its Impact on the Future of Economy and Society

제롬 글렌
(Jerome C. Glenn)

제롬 글렌

Jerome C. Glenn

　밀레니엄 프로젝트(The Millennium Project)의 CEO이자 국제적으로 저명한 미래학자. 1997년 처음 발간되어 현재까지 19권이 발간된 세계미래보고서 시리즈(State of the Future)의 주요 필자로서 지난 40년간 과학·기술, 환경, 경제 등에 대한 미래 연구분야의 글로벌 리더임. 특히 기술발전으로 인하여 급변하는 경제·사회와 관련하여 미래지향적 주제로 300여 회의 강연 및 국제 컨퍼런스에 참여하였으며, 그의 최신 연구는 '세계미래보고서 2020,' 'Work/Technology 2050: Scenarios and Actions' 등의 제목으로 다수 발간됨.

인공지능(AI)이 만드는 경제·사회의 미래

제롬 글렌
미래학자
밀레니엄 프로젝트 CEO

강연을 시작하기에 앞서 강조하고 싶은 점이 있습니다. 기술이 인간을 통제해서는 안 되며 우리가 기술을 통제해야 한다는 것입니다.

우선 모두가 동의하는 점부터 살펴보겠습니다. 인공지능(AI)이 사회에 미치는 영향을 대해 일각에서는 다음과 같이 주장합니다. "농업 시대에서 산업화 시대로, 산업화 시대에서 정보화 시대로 넘어갔을 때에도 다수의 일자리가 사라졌다. 직업의 소멸은 인류 역사의 전환기마다 나타난 현상이다. 이번이라고 다를 바가 없다."

Each economic transition created more jobs than those lost

Why is it different this time?
1. the acceleration of technological change
2. the globalization, interactions, and synergies among NTs
3. the existence of a global platform—the Internet—for simultaneous technology transfer … with far fewer errors in the transfer than in the past
4. standardization of data bases and protocols
5. few plateaus or pauses of change allowing time for individuals and cultures to adjust to the changes
6. billions of empowered people in relatively democratic free markets able to initiate activities
7. machines can learn how you do what you do, and then do it better than you.

그러나 AI의 경우, 변화의 추세가 더 빠르다는 차이가 있습니다. 이것이 첫 번째 변화입니다. AI에 따른 변화가 이전의 변화보다 훨씬 빠르다는 데는 여러분도 동의하실 겁니다. 여러분 조부모의 삶과 현재를 비교해 보십시오. 그동안 큰 변화가 있었습니다. 부모 세대의 삶과 비교해도 마찬가지입니다. 30년 전만 하더라도 한국이 철강 생산량과 이동통신에서 미국을 앞서리라고는 상상조차 할 수 없었습니다. 다른 여러 분야에서도 이처럼 심대한 변화가 나타났습니다. 현재의 기술이 빠르게 변할수록 향후 기술의 발전속도도 증가합니다. 그리고 이 같은 기술 발전의 상승작용에 따라 변화에 가속도가 붙습니다. 지금까지는 볼 수 없었던 모습입니다.

두 번째 변화는 NT입니다. NT의 세계화와 상호작용 및 시너지에 주목해야 합니다. 여기서 NT는 차세대 기술(next technologies)을 가리킵니다. 패킷 교환, 데이터 케이블, 소프트웨어 등의 기술을 일일이 언급하는 대신 ICT라는 약어를 쓰는 것과 마찬가지입니다. 나노 기술, 인지 과학, 합성 생물학을 반복해서 언급하면 번거로우니까 대신 NT라는 용어를 사용하는 거죠. NT의 각 기술은 상호 시너지 효과를 창출합니다. 휴대폰만 하더라도 여러 기술이 녹아 들어가 있습니다. 역시 이전에는 볼 수 없었던 현상입니다. 혹자는 "50년 전에도 세계화는 있었다"고 주장하겠지만 오늘날의 발전에는 미치지 못합니다.

세 번째 변화는 인터넷을 비롯한 글로벌 플랫폼의 존재입니다. 덕분에 정보를 정확하고도 신속하게 전송할 수 있게 되었습니다. 저는 1980년대에 3세계 국가에서 패킷 교환 설비를 설치하는 일을 맡았습니다. 덕분에 사용자들이 인터넷을 저렴하게 이용할 수 있게 되었습니다. 데이터에서 패킷을 생성하여 인공위성을 매개로 전송하는 기술입니다. 이전에는 정보를 주고받으려면 도착지 공항에서 내린 후, 상대방과 전화통화를 하며 의사결정을 내리고 다음 장소로 이동해야 했습니다. 너무 많은 시간이 걸리죠.

인터넷 프로토콜이 개발된 시기가 50년 전입니다. 개발 연도가 1968-69년이니까, 올해가 인터넷 프로토콜 탄생 50주년이 되는 해입니다. 그런데 1990년이 되어서야 이 프로토콜이 본격적으로 이용되기 시작했습니다. 그만큼 기술의 보급에 오랜 시간이 걸렸는데요, 이제는 플랫폼 덕분에 정보를 신속하고 정확하게 보낼 수 있게 되었습니다. 비행기에서 내리면서 통화를 하는 경우, 상대방과 얘기하다가 중요 정보가 기억나지 않을 수도 있습니다. 그러나 이제는 버튼만 누르면 전세계에서 동시에 정보를 받아볼 수 있습니다. 소프트웨어와 데이터 덕분에 가능해진 놀라운 변화입니다.

여러분이 중요한 정보를 입수한다고 합시다. 이제는 그 정보를 모두가 공유할 수 있습니다. 물론 조직 차원에서 집단정보 시스템이 구축되면 그 조직의 구성원 간에는 정보를 교환할 수 있습니다. 이전에는 데이터베이스에 그런 시스템이 없었는데, 이제는 소프트웨어 덕분에 데이터베이스도 공유할 수 있게 되었습니다. 과거에는 불가능했던 일입니다. 데이터베이스의 표준화와 프로토콜 덕분입니다. 이것이 네 번째 변화입니다.

제가 유엔 대학교에서 동경과 워싱턴 사무소 간 연락을 맡은

적이 있습니다. 당시 저는 사람들이 매일 무엇을 먹고 마시는지에 대한 답을 표준화하는 작업을 담당했습니다. 얼핏 원시적이고 단순해 보이지만, 이 같은 표준화를 바탕으로 관련 연구를 수행하며 결과를 학습할 수 있었습니다. 산업화에서 정보화 시대로의 변환기에는 없었던 기술이었습니다.

다섯 번째 변화로는 변화에 적응할 수 있는 시간이 극단적으로 줄어든 점을 꼽을 수 있습니다. 중요하면서도 설명이 쉽지 않은 개념인데요, 저는 1992년에 첫 노트북을 구입했습니다. 지금도 노트북이 있고요. 물론 현재의 노트북 성능은 과거보다 훨씬 더 강력해졌습니다. 그러나 모델은 바뀌었어도 어쨌든 노트북은 노트북이라, 새 모델을 산 후 적응할 시간이 있었습니다. 노트북 외관을 봐도 과거나 지금이나 비슷합니다. 노트북이 갑자기 다른 기기로 교체된 것도 아니고요. 그런데 AI 때문에 노트북이 완전히 바뀌면 변화에 적응하기 어렵습니다. 가령 1992년에 콘택트렌즈가 전혀 다른 도구로 교체되었다고 합시다. 렌즈를 눈에 쓰는 대신 뇌에 이식하는 식입니다. 단기에 익숙해지기에는 너무나 큰 변화입니다. 이처럼 급격하게 기술이 발전하면 사회 차원에서 변화에 적응할 수 있는 시간이 없습니다. 이 역시 과거에는 볼 수 없었던 현상입니다.

다음으로 여섯 번째 변화입니다. 현 경제에서는 민주적 참여가 비교적 잘 보장되어 있기 때문에, 누구나 새로운 아이디어나 발명을 내놓을 수 있습니다. 과거에는 6천만명만 이 같은 변화에 참여할 수 있었다면, 이제는 60억명이 동참할 수 있습니다. 조부모나 부모님 세대와 비교해 보십시오. 당시의 경제에서는 변화에 따라갈 수 있는 시간이 있었습니다. 미래의 변화에 적응할 수 있는 여유가 존재했습니다. 그러나 이제는 전원이 변화의 주역인 시대입니다. 누군가가 새로운 아이디어를 제시하면 실리콘 밸리의 모두가 공유할 수 있습니다. 다음 발명이 나올 때까지 따라잡을 수 있는 시간이 없습니다. 전세계 인구의 절반이 나머지 절반과 인터넷으로 연결되는 세상입니다. 이전에는 없었던 일입니다.

이제 누구나 새로운 운동을 시작할 수 있습니다. 지뢰 금지 협약을 들어보셨는지 모르겠습니다. 미국 메인주의 한 여성은 지뢰 때문에 전세계 아이들이 목숨을 잃는 현실을 두고 볼 수 없다고 결심했습니다. 그런데 지뢰는 비무장 지대 뿐 아니라 전세계 곳곳에 매설되어 있습니다. 그래서 이 여성은 인터넷에서 지뢰 금지에 관해 뜻을 같이 하는 사람들을 찾았습니다. 그리고 이는 지뢰 금지에 관한 국제조약을 체결로 이어졌습니다. 평범한 시민이 단신으로 중대한 변화를 이끌어낸 셈입니다. 우리 모두가 변화의 주역이 될 수 있습니다. 상사의 지시를 수동적으로 따르는 수밖에 없었던 과거와는 크게 달라졌습니다.

마지막 일곱 번째 변화는 기계 학습입니다. 기계는 인간의 학습방식을 배운 후 인간보다 더 효율적으로 작업을 수행할 수 있습니다.

지금까지 7가지의 변화에 대해 말씀드렸습니다. 제가 이 같이 변화를 강조하는데에는 이유가 있습니다. 아직도 "지금의 변화는 과거와 다를 바가 없다. 이전과 마찬가지로 기술의 발전이 새로운 일자리를 창출할 것이다"는 주장을 늘어놓는 이들이 있기 때문입니다. 그러나 앞서의 7가지 변화를 보시면 이 주장이 사실이 아님을 알 수 있습니다. 오늘의 강연에서 다른 내용은 다 잊으셔도 좋습니다. 현재의 변화가 과거에 비해 7가지 측면에서 어떻게 다른지, 그 점만이라도 기억해 주셨으면 합니다.

Inevitability of New Economics, Changing social contract and human rights

- Concentration of wealth is increasing
- Income gaps are widening
- Employmentless economic growth seems the new norm
- Return on Investment in capital and technology is usually better than labor
- Future technologies can replace much of human labor
- Long-term structural unemployment is a "business as usual" or "surprise free" trend forecast
- **What can we do about this?**

다음 슬라이드를 보시겠습니다. 제목이 '신(新)경제의 필연성, 사회 계약의 변화와 인권'입니다. 부의 집중화가 심화되고 있음은 모두가 아실 겁니다. 어느 국가에 살고 있는지, 자본주의나 사회주의 체제 중에서 어디에 속하는지는 중요하지 않습니다. 슬라이드 제목의 변화가 인류 전체 차원에서 나타나고 있습니다. 소득 불평등이 심화되고 일자리 없는 성장이 대세가 되었습니다. 자본 및 투자 수익률이 노동 수익률을 상회하는 시대입니다. 미래의 기술이 인간의 육체노동뿐 아니라 정신 노동까지 대체하는 세상입니다. 장기 구조적 실업은 더 이상 예외적 변수가 아닙니다. 오히려 경제 전망의 일상이 되었습니다. 전세계 인구의 절반이 실업자라면 재앙이나 다름 없는데, 이 같은 재앙적 변화가 놀

랄 것도 없는 시대입니다.

Future Work/Technology 2050 Study

1. Literature and Related Research Review
2. Real-Time Delphi on questions not asked or poorly answered
3. Three Global Scenario Drafts to 2050
4. Three Separate RTDelphi's for Feedback on each Scenario
5. Final Scenarios, given for Millennium Project Nodes
6. National Workshops to Explore Long-range Strategies
7. Collect suggestions from the national planning workshops, distilled in to 93 actions, assess all via five (5) Real-Time Delphi's
8. Final Report for Public Discussion

이 문제를 어떻게 해결할 수 있을까요? 저는 해답을 찾기 위해 관련 논문부터 읽었습니다. 그런데 제가 읽은 30~50여편의 논문에서 합성 생물학을 언급한 논문은 단 하나도 없었습니다. 합성 생물학은 유전자 편집이 아닙니다. 유전자 편집에서는 특정 유전자를 첨가하거나 삭제합니다. 그러나 유전자 편집 후에도 생물 종은 바뀌지 않습니다. 인간은 여전히 인간이고, 닭은 닭으로 남습니다. 장미도 마찬가지입니다.

합성 생물학은 다릅니다. 컴퓨터를 이용해서 기존에는 없었던 종을 만들 수도 있고 새로운 능력을 생성할 수 있습니다. 이 새로운 능력이란 뇌의 혈전 제거일 수도 있고 바다 청소일 수도 있습니다. 그 외 어떤 작업이라도 가능합니다. 합성 생물학에서는 연구자가 컴퓨터 화면을 보며 완전히 상이한 종들의 유전자를 합성합니다. 이 과정을 통해 탄생한 합성물을 테스트한 후 제품으로 판매합니다. 전세계의 주요 합성생물학 업체 중 하나가 홍콩 소재의 GenScript라는 회사입니다. 제가 이 회사의 주식을 보유하고 있는데요, GenScript로부터 합성물을 조합하여 새로운 생물학적 특성을 구현할 수 있습니다. 과거에는 창조주만 가능했던 작업을 이제는 인간도 해낼 수 있게 되었습니다.

뇌를 중심으로 합성 생물학을 설명해 보겠습니다. 여러분이 미생물을 합성한 후 뇌에 이식한다고 합시다. 이 미생물은 뇌혈관의 혈전을 제거합니다. 덕분에 99세 노인의 뇌를 25세 젊은이의 뇌로 되돌릴 수 있습니다. 고령화 시대에 유용한 기술입니다. 고령화의 경제적 영향은 여러분도 아실 겁니다. 노인 인구의 증가로 은퇴자와 환자 수가 늘면 언젠가는 경제가 파탄에 빠집니다. 그런데 합성생물학 덕분에 우리가 건강과 인지능력을 유지한다면 나이가 들어도 은퇴하지 않고 계속 일할 수 있습니다. 세금도 납부할 수 있습니다. 국가재정에 부담이 되지 않고 오히려 기여하게 됩니다. 뇌가 쇠퇴하면 상당수의 다른 신체 기능도 상실된다는 점을 감안할 때, 혈전 제거로 뇌의 노화를 늦출 수 있다면 그 영향은 대단히 클 것입니다.

아니면 청소만 하는 새로운 종을 합성할 수도 있습니다. 이 생명체는 직원들이 퇴근한 후 청소를 시작합니다. 몇 시간동안 건물을 청소한 후 먼지를 모아서 다른 곳에 버립니다. 진공 청소기가 필요 없습니다. 진공 청소기를 판매하는 영업 사원도 사라집니다. 전기료도 낼 일이 없습니다. 쓰레기도 나오지 않습니다. 물론 청소하면서 쓰레기가 발생하기는 하겠지만 합성 생물학 덕분에 쓰레기를 압축 처리할 수 있습니다.

한마디로 합성 생물학은 산업 혁명보다 더 큰 변화를 촉발할 수 있습니다. 그럼에도 제가 읽은 30~50편의 논문에서는 이 분야를 전혀 언급하지 않고 있습니다. 그래서 저와 당사의 직원들은 합성 생물학을 직접 연구했습니다. 합성 생물학은 막대한 경제적 잠재력을 지니고 있습니다. 향후 경제 성장과 일자리 창출의 원천이 될 것입니다.

저희는 합성 생물학처럼 그 잠재력에도 불구하고 충분한 주목을 받지 못한 분야를 파악한 후, 관련 설문지를 작성했습니다. 예컨대 상당수 논문에서는 STEM(이공계) 교육의 강화가 답이라고 주장합니다. 그런데 전세계 60억 명의 인구 중에서 과학기술이나 공학으로 생계를 꾸릴 수 있는 사람은 소수에 불과합니다. 이공계를 전공하지 않은 나머지가 문제됩니다. 저희가 설문지를 작성한 이유도 이 문제에 대한 답을 찾기 위해서였습니다. 우선 설문지를 작성해서 전세계에 산재한 65개의 노드에 입력했습니다. 이 노드들은 누구를 상대로 설문조사를 실시해야 할지 분석작업을 수행했습니다. 예컨대 이란에서 이공계 교육의 전문가가 누구인지 저는 모르기 때문에 노드에 설문 대상자의 파악을 맡긴 것입니다. 노드의 분석이 끝나면 설문 결과를 취합해서 3개의 시나리오 초안을 작성합니다. 작성된 시나리오 초안은 다시 한 번 노드의 분석작업을 거친 후 시나리오를 개선하는 데 활용됩니다. 이 과정을 통해 시나리오의 개연성을 높일 수 있었습니다.

시나리오의 역할에 대해 잠시 말씀드리겠습니다. 현재 전세계에서 이루어지는 시나리오 작성 방식에 큰 문제가 있는 것은 아닙니다. 적어도 없는 것보다는 낫습니다. 그러나 우리가 시나리오를 작성하는 목적은 가장 가능성이 높은 미래를 점치는 것이 아닙니다. 당연히 인지했어야 함에도 간과한 점은 없는지 파악하기 위해서입니다. 무지하다는 점조차 몰랐던 사실을 깨닫는 것입니다. 시나리오를 처음 작성한 기관은 미국의 RAND 연구소입니다. 목적은 제3차 세계대전의 가능성을 전망하기 위해서였습니다. 그전까지는 전사(戰史)학자들이 이런 저런 분석을 했지만, 대부분은 단정적인 전망에 그쳤습니다. 열핵전쟁이 일어나면 인류가 파멸하리라는 식이었습니다. 주요 분석도구는 리스크 평가로, 각 리스크 상황에 대한 전망을 내놓는 식이었습니다.

RAND에서는 이 같은 분석에 한계를 느끼고 무에서부터 시나리오를 작성하기 시작했습니다. 스토리 식으로 시나리오를 작성함으로써 그동안 간과된 요소를 찾고자 했습니다. 그렇다고 격자형의 표를 만들어서 각 시나리오별 상황을 예측한다는 소리는 아닙니다. 중요한 것은 시나리오의 결과가 아니라 작성 과정을 살펴봄으로써 결과와 원인의 연결고리를 찾는 것입니다. 이를 통해 그동안 미처 파악하지 못했던 점을 발견할 수 있습니다. 이것이 시나리오를 작성하는 이유입니다. 그 점에서 시나리오를 작성하는 작업은 외주를 주어서는 안 됩니다. 작성을 의뢰 받은 SF 작가만 공부하고, 정작 의뢰인은 아무것도 배우지 못하기 때문입니다.

시나리오는 내부 직원이 써야 합니다. 직원 입에서 "잘 모르겠습니다"라는 말이 나올 때까지 시나리오를 다듬어야 합니다. 예컨대 당사의 직원이 작성한 시나리오에는 기본소득에 대한 전망치가 들어가 있었습니다. 저는 이 직원에게 시나리오상에서 언제까지 기본소득을 지급할 수 있는지 물어보았습니다. 이를 위해서는 미래 현금흐름에 대한 분석이 필요했습니다. 현금흐름 예측은 경영 현장에서 많이 쓰이는 분석 도구입니다. 그런데 기존의 연구 중에서는 현금흐름 예측을 포함한 연구가 전무했습니다. 더구나 제가 질문하기 전에는 누구도 이 사실을 깨닫지 못했습니다. 저희 뿐 아니라 스위스나 핀란드 학자들도 마찬가지였습니다. 기본소득의 지속가능성을 가늠하려면 현금흐름 전망이 필수적임에도, 이에 필요한 분석도구를 갖추지 못한 것입니다. 다행히 시나리오를 작성하며 미비점을 파악한 덕분에, 현금흐름 분석을 시나리오에 추가할 수 있었습니다.

시나리오 작성이 끝나면, 전세계의 노드가 이를 검토합니다. 여러분도 이 검토에 참여할 수 있습니다. 이 작업의 취지는 다양한 가능성을 탐색하는 것입니다. 누구도 미래를 단언할 수는 없습니다. 적어도 제대로 된 미래학자라면 자신이 미래를 정확히 예측할 수 있다고 주장하지 않습니다. 서울의 마른 하늘에 갑자기 날벼락이 떨어져서 모든 것이 바뀔 가능성도 전적으로 배제할 수는 없기 때문입니다.

미래를 확실하게 전망할 수는 없습니다. 그러나 여러 가능성은 살펴볼 수 있습니다. 우리가 다양한 시나리오를 작성하는 이유는 '앞으로 X 사건이 일어날 것이다'고 전망하기 위해서가 아닙니다. X를 포함한 다양한 가능성을 고려함으로써 현재 필요한 대책을 강구하기 위해서입니다. 실제로 저희는 워크숍 등을 통해 여러 국가에 대한 시나리오를 작성하고 시나리오별 대응책도 제시했습니다. 관심있는 분은 오늘 행사장에 비치한 책자를 보시면 됩니다.

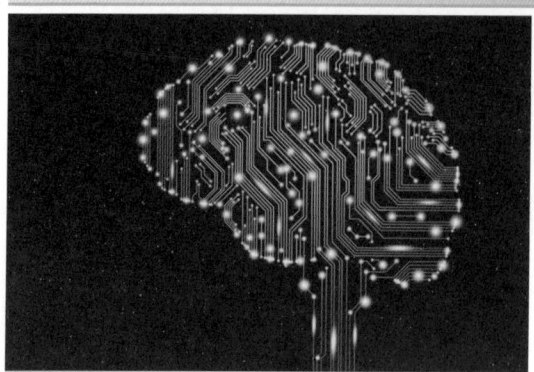

Three Forms of Artificial Intelligence

- Artificial Narrow Intelligence
- Artificial General Intelligence
- Artificial Super Intelligence

다음은 AI입니다. AI에는 3개의 유형이 있습니다. 그런데 유감스럽게도 각 유형별 구분이 명확하지 않아 의사결정에 혼란이 발생하고 있습니다. AI에는 협의의 AI(narrow AI), 범용 AI(general AI), 초고성능 AI(super AI)가 있습니다. AI를 얘기할 때 어느 유형을 말하는지 분명히 해야 합니다.

많은 한국인은 알파고를 보고 인공지능의 시대가 도래했다고 얘기합니다. 실제로 협의의 AI는 이미 현실화되었습니다. 그러나 협의의 AI는 공상과학 영화에 등장하는 초고성능 AI가 아닙니다. 협의의 AI로 이미 자율주행차 운전이나 암의 진단은 가능해졌습니다. 반면 범용 인공지능의 실현은 훨씬 더 난이도가 높습니다. 어쩌면 영원히 현실화되지 못할 수도 있습니다. 미래는 항상 우리의 예상을 뛰어넘었습니다. 하지만 미래학자는 의심할 여지 없이 확실히 범용 AI가 등장할 것이라고 단언하지는 않습니다. 그럼에도 굳이 전망을 하자면, 이는 실현되지 못할 수도 있고, 실현될 수도 있다고 말씀드려야 하겠습니다. 심지어는 10-15년 내에 현실화될 가능성도 있습니다.

범용 AI는 자율주행차 운전, 암 진단, 일정 관리 등 여러 작업을 수행할 수 있습니다. 더 나아가 사물인터넷(IoT)을 비롯한 협의의 AI 처리능력도 활용할 수 있습니다. 사람이 문제를 풀다가 모르는 점이 있으면 자료조사를 하거나 타인에게 질문하는 것처럼, 범용 AI도 문제해결 과정에서 의문점이 생기면 인간에게 물어볼 수 있습니다. 이 과정에서 발생한 모든 정보는 공동의 플랫폼에서 공유됩니다. 덕분에 한 도시에서 솔루션을 발견하면 다른 도시들도 이를 실시간으로 접할 있습니다. 그 결과 경이적인 수준의 AI 발전이 가능해집니다.

AI 얘기가 나올 때마다 이공계 교육의 중요성이 강조되는데, 협의의 AI에서는 맞는 말입니다. 그러나 2030-35년에 범용 AI가 실현되면 이공계 교육도 무용지물이 됩니다. 범용 AI와 협의의 AI는 인간과 개만큼의 격차가 있습니다. 다른 대상에 빗대자면, 인터넷과 팩시밀리만큼의 차이가 존재합니다. 인터넷과 팩스 모두 정보화 시대의 산물입니다. 그러나 둘의 성능은 차원이 다릅니다. 그런데 인터넷과 팩스의 성능 차는 알면서도 협의의 AI와 범용 AI는 제대로 구분하지 못하는 것 같습니다. 실제로 둘을 혼동하는 모습을 자주 볼 수 있습니다.

푸틴이 "AI를 정복하는 국가가 세계를 지배한다"고 말할 때, 여기서의 AI는 협의의 AI가 아닙니다. 푸틴 본인은 의식하지 못할 수도 있지만 범용 AI를 의미합니다. 그리고 중국이 "중국제조 2025(中国制造2025)" 계획을 발표했을 때 어떤 AI에서 선두주자가 되겠다는 것인지 확실하지는 않지만, 아마도 범용 AI가 아닐까 싶습니다. 사실이라면 상당히 의미심장한 목표입니다.

초고성능(super) 인공지능은 인간의 개입 없이 컴퓨터 스스로 목표를 세울 수 있습니다. 그래서 super라는 수식어가 붙습니다. 공상과학 영화에 등장하는 유형의 인공지능입니다. 엘론 머스크가 말하는 인공지능이자 인간이 우려하는 인공지능이기도 합니다. 그런데 범용 AI조차 당분간은 실현 가능성이 없고 초고성능 AI는 그 이후에야 등장할 수 있다면, 왜 벌써부터 걱정을 하는 것일까요?

Next Technologies (NT): Imagine How NT Synergies Will Create New Businesses

- Artificial Intelligence
- Robotics
- Synthetic Biology & Genomics
- Computational Science
- Cloud & Big Data Analytics
- Artificial & Augmented Reality
- Nanotechnology (two kinds)
- IoT, Tele-Everything & Tele-Everybody, the Semantic Web
- Quantum computing
- Tele-Presence, Holographic Communications
- Intelligence augmentation
- Collective Intelligence
- Blockchain
- 3D/4D Printing Materials/Biology
- Drones, Driverless Cars (and other autonomous vehicles)
- Conscious-Technology
- **Synergies Among These**

그 이유는 범용 AI에서 초고성능 AI로 넘어가는 데 걸리는 시간을 알 수 없기 때문입니다. 바로 다음 순간일수도 있고, 그 시기가 영원히 오지 않을 수도 있습니다. 즉 미지의 영역입니다. 그래도 미래학자로서 내기를 건다면 저는 초 인공지능이 실현된다는 쪽에 베팅을 하겠습니다. 그러나 정확한 시기까지 예상하지는 않겠습니다. 범용 AI가 도래하기 전에 먼저 AI의 기준부터 세워야 합니다. 만일 AI에 대한 합의나 기준이나 초기 조건 없이 범용 AI와 마주하게 되면, 인간이 AI를 통제할 수 없게 됩니다. 그 합의나 기준의 마련에 상당한 시간이 걸리기 때문에, AI에 대한 우려가 나오는 것입니다. 그래서 인공지능에 관한 합의를 이루는 작업은 지금부터 시작해야 합니다.

우리가 NT의 도래에 주목하는 이유는 각각의 기술이 큰 잠재력을 갖고 있기 때문입니다. 유전학의 합성 생물학에 대해서는 이미 말씀드렸습니다. 컴퓨터 공학에서도 과거에는 각 연구소마다 독자적으로 연산을 했다면, 이제는 작업의 동시 수행이 가능해졌습니다. 덕분에 기술의 발전에 가속도가 붙었습니다. 여러분들도 잘 아시는 클라우드 컴퓨팅이나 데이터는 예측 분석에 많이 쓰이고 있습니다. 나노 기술도 있습니다. 거대한 장비를 동원해서 미세한 공정을 실현하는 기술입니다. 그러나 기술의 진정한 잠재력은 다른 데 있습니다. 기술이 실현되는 규모를 점점 키우는 것입니다. 식물의 잎을 보면 그 자체가 정밀 공업이라고 할 수 있습니다. 잎은 열을 발생시키지 않고도 수소와 산소를 분리할 수 있는데, 인간의 현존 나노 기술로는 아직 구현할 수 없는 기능입니다. 나노 기술이 더 발전해야 식물의 잎 수준에서 수소와 산소를 분리할 수 있습니다. 현재의 AI를 넘는 수준의 기술입니다. IoT나 모든 것이 소통하는(tele-everything)하는 기술도 있습니다.

다음은 양자(量子, quantum) 컴퓨터입니다. 양자 컴퓨터를 무료로 이용할 수 있다는 점을 알고 계신가요? 이 자리에서 그 사실을 처음 알게 된 분도 계실 텐데요, 물론 무료로 이용할 수 있는 양자 컴퓨터의 성능은 5 큐비트(qubit) 수준으로 아직 제한적입니다. 그러나 어쨌든 양자 컴퓨터인 점은 사실이고, IBM이 개발한 컴퓨터입니다. D-Wave(캐나다의 하드웨어 기업)에서도 양자 컴퓨터를 개발하여 판매하고 있습니다. 가격이 상당히 높기는 하지만요. 양자 컴퓨터에 대해서는 각자 이견이 있을 수 있지만, 적어도 더 이상은 미래학자의 전망에서만 존재하는 기술은 아닙니다. 아직 초기 단계이지만 실존하는 기술입니다. 다만 왜 양자 컴퓨터가 막강한 잠재력을 갖는지 이 자리에서 설명하기는 어렵습니다. 사실 설명이 불가능하다고 할 수 있습니다. 양자 컴퓨터를 이해하려면 양자 역학부터 알아야 하기 때문입니다. 결론부터 말씀드리자면, 양자 컴퓨터 덕분에 과거보다 훨씬 빠른 계산이 가능해집니다. 그래서 암호화 기술이 무용지물이 됩니다. 양자 컴퓨터로 암호를 걸지 않는 한 말이죠. 양자 컴퓨터는 많은 잠재력을 가진 기술입니다. 일정 시간이 지나야 그 잠재력이 실현되겠지만, 중요한 기술임에는 분명합니다.

다음으로 원격 현장감(tele-presence), 홀로그래픽 통신, 증강 지능, 집단 지능, 블록체인, 3D/4D 프린팅, 드론, 무인 자동차, 기타 자율 주행차, 의식 기술 등이 슬라이드에 나와 있습니다. 그리고 이들 기술이 모여 시너지를 이룰 수 있습니다. 그 시너지가 바로 NT입니다. ICT가 소프트웨어와 하드웨어의 시너지인 것과 마찬가지입니다. 이 시너지에 주목해야 합니다. 일각에서는 AI가 차세대 기술의 전부라고 생각하는데, 단지 AI만이 아닙니다. 여기 나온 모든 기술 및 각 기술 간의 시너지가 NT의 진정한 모습입니다.

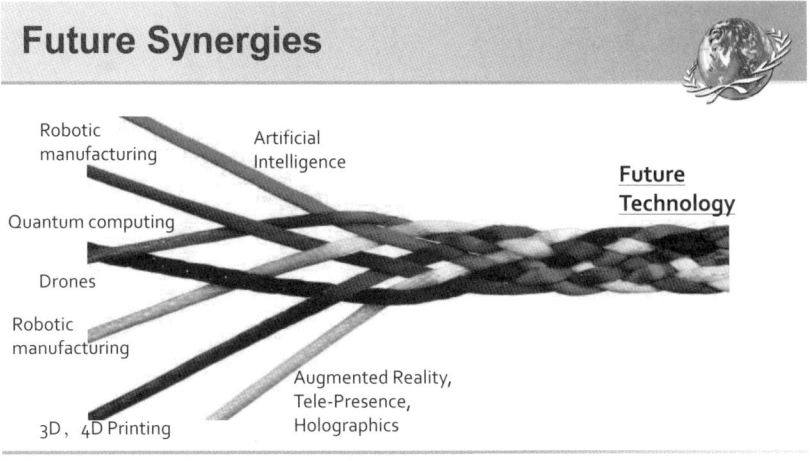

이 자리에 경제학자도 계신 것으로 알고 있는데요, 경제학에서 말하는 부의 창출이란 여러 요소를 결합하여 기존에 존재하지 않았던 새로운 발명을 이룩하는 것입니다. 우리가 목격하고 있는 기술의 발전도 이 같은 결합에서 나옵니다. 과거보다 빠른 속도로 발전이 이루어지고 있습니다.

이 슬라이드는 기존의 기술에 대한 시각을 나타냅니다. 각각의 기술이 별개로 존재한다고 인식하는 것입니다. 그러나 이는 잘못된 인식입니다. 지금 같은 기술의 발전을 예상하지 못했다면, 이는 발전의 한 면만 보고 다른 면까지는 보지 않았기 때문입니다. 그러나 우리는 기술의 통합과 시너지 시대에 살고 있습니다. 정육면체 퍼즐을 맞추는 과정을 생각하시면 됩니다. 큐빅 퍼즐처럼 기술을 통합하는 과정에서 새로운 아이디어가 탄생합니다. 새로운 아이디어가 탄생하지 않는 것이 오히려 불가능하다고 할 수 있습니다. 믿기지 않는다면 직접 시도해 보십시오. 가령 나노 기술이 합성 생물학에 가지는 함의를 생각해 보는 식입니다. 아직까지 두 기술이 결합된 적이 없는데, 이 두 기술을 통합할 때의 결과를 상상해 보는 겁니다. 분명 새로운 아이디어가 탄생합니다. 단지 그 지점까지 우리의 생각이 미치지 못했을 뿐입니다. 여기 슬라이드처럼 이 기술들을 한 가닥으로 묶을 수도 있습니다.

Work/Tech Global Scenarios 2050

Each scenario is about 10 pages of detailed cause & effect sequences that illustrate decisions

1. It's Complicated - A Mixed Bag

2. Political/Economic Turmoil – Future Despair

3. If Humans Were Free – The Self-Actualizing Economy

당사는 이 같은 기술의 결합을 3개의 시나리오로 정리했습니다. 이 시나리오를 기초로 기술 발전에 대한 각자의 생각을 나눌 수 있습니다. 시나리오에 관한 자료를 오늘 행사장에 비치했는데, 오늘은 무료로 가져가실 수 있지만 나중에는 돈을 주고 구입하셔야 할 겁니다. 그런데 가급적이면 책자가 아니라 전자파일로 자료를 받으시기를 권합니다. 키워드 검색도 쉽고, 저희도 책자를 우편으로 배송할 필요가 없기 때문입니다. 어쨌든 각 시나리오가 10페이지 정도 되는데, "가정-전망(if-then)"으로 이루어져 있습니다. 변화의 각 단계를 전망하다가 지금껏 몰랐던 부분이 나오면, 시나리오 읽기를 멈추고 해당 부분을 찾아보시면 됩니다.

첫 번째 시나리오는 "복잡한 복합적 미래(It's Complicated-A Mixed Bag)"입니다. 저희가 2050년까지 전망한 데는 나름의 이유가 있습니다. 다른 미래학자의 전망을 보면 대개 향후 5년이나 10년 뒤를 예측합니다. 그런데 5년은 문화의 변화를 파악하기에 부족한 기간입니다. 경제 시스템의 변화도 마찬가지입니다. 전술한 여러 기술이 결합되면 문화적으로나 경제적으로나 큰 영향을 미칠 것입니다. 그런데 그 효과를 제대로 가늠하려면 이보다 더 멀리 내다보아야 합니다. 이것이 저희가 2050년까지의 시나리오를 작성한 이유입니다. 미래의 변화에 선제적으로 대응할 수 있도록 충분한 여유를 두는 겁니다. 상당수 변화는 오랜 시간을 들여야 해법을 찾을 수 있기 때문입니다. 지금부터 그 변화를 전망해야만 미리 대비할 수 있습니다. 그런데 변화의 가속화에 추가로 가속도가 붙으면, 2050년 시점에는 우리가 몰라볼 정도로 큰 변화가 나타날 수 있습니다. 저는 현재의 발전 추세가 미래에도 계속된다(business as usual)고 전망한다고 있습니다.

다음 시나리오는 "정치/경제적 혼란 - 암울한 미래(Political/Economic Turmoil - Future Despair)"입니다. 이 시나리오는 잠시 뒤에 설명 드리겠습니다. 세 번째 시나리오에서는 모든 것이 실현됩니다. 만일 여러분이 철저한 비관주의자라면 세 번째 시나리오를 읽으시기를 권합니다. 지나친 낙관주의자라면 두 번째 시나리오를 읽으시고요. 좀 더 냉정하게 현실을 직시할 수 있게 될 겁니다. 그만큼 시나리오 2는 비관적입니다. 그러나 3개 시나리오 모두 충분한 개연성이 있습니다. 물론 각각의 시나리오는 현재까지 많은 논쟁의 대상이 되었으며, 이 시나리오처럼 미래가 펼쳐진다고 제가 단언하는 것은 아닙니다. 그러나 개연성은 있다는 점을 말씀드리고 싶습니다.

Global Employment Assumptions
Workforce 3 billion 2000; 6 billion 2050

	Scenario 1 Business as Usual	Scenario 2 Political Turmoil	Scenario 3 Self-Actualization
Employed	2 Billion	1 Billion	1 Billion
Self-Employed	2 Billion	1 Billion	3 Billion
Unemployed or in transition	1 Billion	2 Billion	1 Billion
Informal Economy	1 Billion	2 Billion	1 Billion

이들 시나리오는 어디까지나 가정입니다. 경제 전망과는 다릅니다. 양자 간의 차이에 유념해야 합니다. 일단 시나리오 1부터 보겠습니다. 이 시나리오에서 20억명은 과거와 같은 방식으로 일합니다. 회사에서 상사의 지시를 받으며 일하고, 그 대가로 월급을 받는 피고용인(employed)입니다. 다음으로 자기 고용(self-employed)입니다. 현재의 변화 트렌드가 계속된다면, 2050년 시점에서는 자영업자의 수가 크게 늘어나 20억명에 이를 것입니다. 다음 10억명은 실업 상태이거나 고용의 전환기에 있는 사람들입니다. 그리고 경제의 비공식 부문에 종사하는 인구가 10억명에 이르게 됩니다. 미래에도 비공식 부문이 완전히 사라지지는 않을 것입니다.

이집트만 보더라도 비공식 부문이 경제에서 차지하는 비중이 60%에 달합니다. 오늘 이 자리에 주한 이집트 대사님도 오신 것으로 아는데요. 저기 계시는군요. 정말로 비공식 부문의 비중이 60%인지 확실하게 알 수는 없다고 말씀하시네요. 저도 같은 생각입니다. 확실한 수치는 알 수 없습니다. 그러나 추정은 할 수 있겠죠. 적어도 상당수 인원이 비공식 부문에서 일하는 것은 사실입니다. 이집트처럼 비공식 경제의 규모가 큰 나라에서 그 비중을 줄이는 것은 아주 어려운 일입니다. 이집트만이 아니라 다른 국가도 마찬가지입니다. 심지어 가장 낙관적인 시나리오 3에서도 여전히 10억명이 비공식 부문에서 일하리라고 전망합니다. 비공식 경제도 엄연히 경제의 일부로서 많은 경제활동이 이루어집니다. 다만 공식통계에 잡히지 않고 과세 대상도 아니라는 차이가 있습니다.

시나리오 2에서는 피고용인이 10억명, 자기 고용자의 수가 10억명, 실업자가 20억명, 비공식 부문 종사자가 20억명입니다. 2000년의 노동인구는 30억명이었습니다. 2050년의 노동인구는 60억명이라고 합시다. 전체 인구가 아니라 노동인구입니다. 시나리오 1에서는 피고용인과 자기 고용인의 수가 각각 20억명으로, 합치면 40억명입니다. 시나리오 2보다 일하는 사람의 수가 많습니다. 시나리오 3에서도 일자리가 있는 사람의 수가 40억명입니다. 다만 피고용인이 10억명, 자기 고용자가 30억명으로 비중이 다를 뿐입니다. 반면 시나리오 2에서는 일자리가 있는 사람의 수가 20억명에 그칩니다. 즉 시나리오 1과 3에 비해 일자리 수가 적은 셈입니다.

Scenario 1:

It's Complicated – A Mixed Bag

- A business-as-usual trend projection
- Increasing acceleration of change with both intelligence and stupidity
- Irregular adoption of advance technology
- Major employment growth in Biotech Industries
- High unemployment where governments did not create long-range strategies
- Mixed success on the use of universal basic income.
- Giant corporations grow beyond government control, in this government-corporate, virtual-3D, multi-polar world of 2050.

시나리오 1에서는 변화의 가속화가 계속되리라고 전망합니다. 이 변화에는 바람직한 변화도 있고 그렇지 못한 변화도 있습니다. 바람직한 변화의 예로는 바이오 산업에서의 일자리 창출을 들 수 있습니다. 바람직하지 못한 변화로의 예로는 첨단 기술을 체계적으로 수용하지 못하거나, 실업률이 높거나, 정부의 장기전략 부재 등을 들 수 있습니다 예컨대 30~40년 전만 하더라도 가나와 한국 경제는 비슷한 처지에 놓여 있었습니다. 그런데 이후 한국 경제에는 바람직한 변화가 일어났습니다. 한국 정부는 장기 경제성장 전략을 세웠습니다. 멀리 내다보고 정책을 운용했습니다. 반면 가나에는 이 같은 장기전략이 없었습니다. 그 외 시나리오 1에서는 기본소득의 효과가 국가별로 다르게 나타납니다. 대기업은 정부가 손을 쓸 수 없을 정도로 커집니다. 시나리오 1에서는 2050년에 기업과 3D 기술의 비중이 늘어나고 세계가 다극체제의 양상을 띱니다.

미래에는 손동작이나 핸드폰, 노트북 없이도 AI를 이용하여 각종 사물을 조작할 수 있습니다. 콘텍트 렌즈를 비롯한 이러한 사물은 3D 프린터로 제작됩니다. 현재도 3D 프린터를 이용한 생산이 실험적으로 이루어지고 있습니다. 정확한 업체명은 기억나지 않지만, 이미 한국의 한 기업에서는 클릭 한 번만으로 사진을

찍어 인터넷으로 전송할 수 있는 콘텍트 렌즈를 개발했습니다. 미래에도 물리적 공간과 가상현실(VR)의 구분은 남겠지만, 이 구분은 큰 의미가 없을 겁니다. 인터넷의 등장 후에도 전화기와 컴퓨터가 별개의 기기로서 존속했지만, 둘의 경계가 허물어진 것과 마찬가지입니다. 2050년이면 인간의 물리적 신체가 안드로이드나 홀로그램, 플래시 등 다양한 형태로 구현되는 등 물리적 공간과 가상 공간이 혼재된 모습을 보일 것입니다.

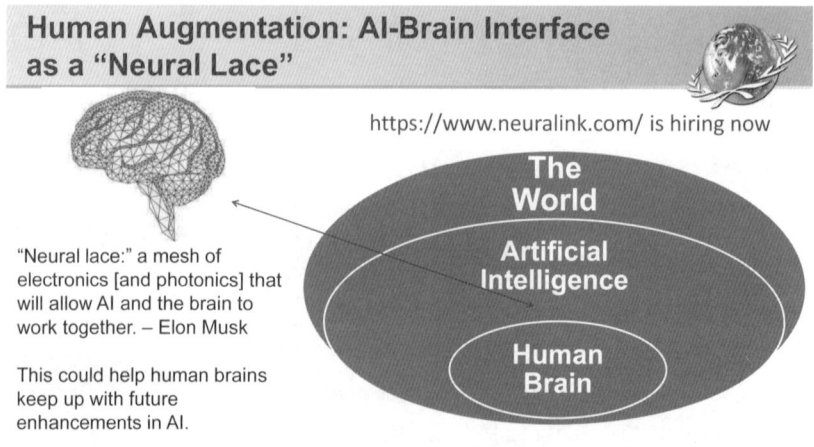

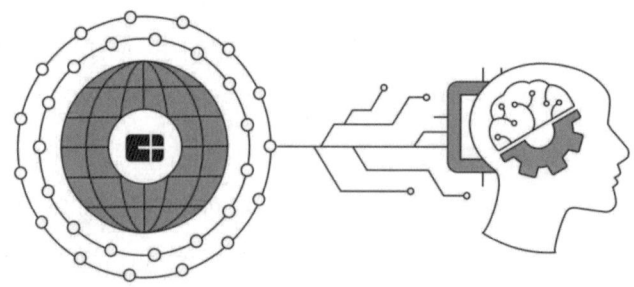

Source CBINSIGHTS

엘론 머스크의 기업에서는 직경이 머리카락의 50분의 1에 불과한 전극을 제작하여 로봇으로 뇌에 이식했습니다. 이제 인간의 뇌를 인터넷과 연결하는 것도 더 이상 꿈이 아닙니다. 오히려 미래의 트렌드가 될 것입니다. 가령 IQ 테스트를 할 때, 패턴 인식 소프트웨어를 이용해 문제를 분석해서 만점을 기록하는 것도 가능해집니다. 마치 안경 없이는 시력 검사에 떨어지는 사람도, 안경을 써서 시력 검사를 통과하는 것과 마찬가지입니다. 미래에는 증강 지능이 현실화되고, 모든 작업에 로봇이 통합될 것입니다. 이것이 시나리오 1의 트렌드 전망입니다.

Scenario 2:

Political/Economic Turmoil – Future Despair

- Political grid-lock increases social polarization, prevents decisionmaking
- Political, economic, environmental migrations increase ethnic conflicts
- Governments did not anticipate impacts of artificial <u>general</u> intelligence: hence, no strategies to address increasing mass unemployment
- Unemployment exploded in the 2030s leads to 2050 in political turmoil
- Financial systems cannot support ageing societies, financial crises
- World order has deteriorated into a combination of nation-states, mega-corporations, local militias, terrorist groups, and organized crime

다음은 시나리오 2입니다. 여기서는 시나리오 1과 다른 가정을 하게 됩니다. 정보전 때문에 성향과 이념별로 사회적 분열이 일어난다는 가정입니다. 정보전은 러시아만 수행하는 것이 아닙니다. 러시아는 미국에 사이비 공격을 하고도 아무런 제재를 받지 않았는데, 이를 보고 다른 국가와 기업도 정보전에 뛰어들 수 있습니다. X 국가 시민이나 Y국가 지도자 모두 정보전의 비용과

효과를 계산하게 됩니다. 정보전은 전차 등을 동원한 실제 전쟁보다 비용이 훨씬 적게 듭니다. 환경 파괴의 영향도 작습니다. 그러나 정보전은 인간을 편집증적 상태로 몰아넣을 수 있습니다. 생물학적 편집증이 아닌 행태적 편집증입니다. 편집증이라 함은 서로를 믿지 못한다는 얘기입니다. 사회는 정치적 교착상태에 빠집니다. AI 등의 중요한 기술은 글로벌 차원의 합의를 필요로 합니다. 그런데 상호 불신 때문에 합의를 보지 못한다면, 예컨대 다른 국가에서는 AI에 대해 올바른 결정을 내리는 반면 일본은 잘못된 선택을 하는 상황이 나타날 수 있습니다. 그리고 우리는 이 같은 선택의 대가를 치르게 됩니다.

시나리오 2에서는 상호간 불신으로 말미암아 정치·경제·환경 문제를 둘러싼 분쟁이 나타납니다. 이 분쟁 때문에 인종 간 갈등과 인구 이동이 일어납니다. 실제로 강제 이주민은 대부분 분쟁 지역에서 발생합니다. 지구 인구의 절반은 실업자이고 절반은 강제 이주민인 경우를 상상해 보십시오. 지금의 난민 문제보다 훨씬 더 심각한 위기가 일어날 것입니다.

지금까지 각국 정부는 협의의 AI에만 신경 썼습니다. 인공지능 때문에 트럭 운전사가 일자리를 잃으리라는 식이었습니다. 그러나 협의의 AI에서는 하루아침에 로봇이 모든 인간을 대체하지는 않습니다. 그래서 사전 대비가 가능합니다. 반면 범용 AI는 다릅니다. 범용 AI가 실현되면 대량의 실업자 발생 등 근본적 변화가 나타납니다. 지난 달이나 작년까지만 해도 실업률이 10%였는데 갑자기 50%로 치솟는 식입니다. 그 결과 사회적으로 큰 혼란이 나타날 것입니다. 이러한 범용 AI에 대해 어떤 정부도 대응 전략을 마련하지 못했습니다.

　시나리오 2에서는 2030년이나 2050년경에 실업률이 폭발적으로 증가합니다. 이는 정치적 혼란으로 이어집니다. 기존의 금융 시스템은 고령화된 인구를 더 이상 지탱하지 못합니다. 그래서 여러 방향에서 금융 위기가 발생합니다. 기존의 세계 질서는 무너지고 국가, 대기업, 지역 반군, 범죄조직 등 여러 행위자가 혼재되는 양상을 띱니다. 만일 지나친 낙관주의자라면 이 시나리오 2를 읽으시기를 권합니다. 찬물을 끼얹는 듯한 느낌을 받으실 수 있을 겁니다.

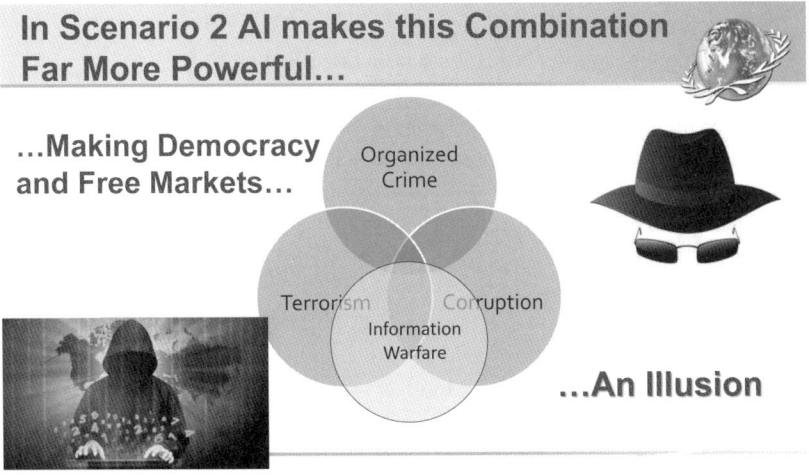

　범죄 조직의 연수입은 각국 국방비의 2배에 달합니다. 상당히 높은 수치입니다. 전세계의 군사비는 연간 1.6~1.7조 달러 정도 됩니다. 반면 범죄 조직의 수익은 3~4조 달러 수준입니다. 범죄 조직은 막강한 자금력을 바탕으로 아낌없이 조직원을 고용하고 장비를 사들일 수 있습니다. 이는 심각한 문제입니다. 범죄조

직이 돈을 무기로 앞서 말씀드린 NT를 활용한다고 상상해 보십시오. 현재의 NT 관련 문제가 미래에는 훨씬 더 심각해질 것입니다. 조직 범죄와 테러리즘, 부패는 정보전과 더불어 중대한 위협입니다. 자칫하면 민주주의와 자유 시장경제가 유명무실해질 수도 있습니다.

Scenario 3:
If Humans Were Free
the Self-Actualization Economy

- Governments did anticipate the impacts of artificial general intelligence
- Conducted extensive research on how to phase in universal basic income systems
- Increasing intelligence becomes a goal of education
- Self-employment promoted
- Artists, media moguls, and entertainers helped to foster cultural change from an employment culture to a self-actualization economy.

다음은 시나리오 3입니다. 이 시나리오에서는 모든 문제가 잘 해결됩니다. 정부에서는 AI의 영향을 예측해서 대응 전략을 마련합니다. 기본소득을 도입하기 전에 철저한 연구조사를 거칩니다. 지적능력 향상이 교육의 주요 목표가 됩니다. 아이가 3세에서 5세 사이에 충분한 철분과 단백질을 섭취하지 못하면 뇌가 제대로 성장하지 못합니다. 북한의 만성적인 기아를 생각하시면 이해가 쉬울 겁니다. 독일 통일의 경우, 당시 동독은 통일 전 50년 동안 북한과 같은 기아를 겪지 않았습니다. 그럼에도 통일 후 상당한 비용이 발생했습니다. 그 점에서 한국은 독일보다도 훨씬 더 어려운 상황에 놓여 있으며, 증강 지능의 필요성을 진지하게 검토할 필요가 있습니다. 지금부터 준비하지 않으면 나중에 큰 문제가 될 것입니다.

다음으로 자기고용 노동자(self-employed)의 이미지 개선입니다. 이 시나리오의 주요 변수 중 하나인데요. 기존의 고용문화에서 벗어나 자기고용 노동자로 일하며 자아를 실현하는 문화로 전환해야 합니다. 이 과정에서 예술가, 미디어 회사, 연예인들의 홍보가 중요합니다. 현대 사회에서는 직업이 곧 정체성입니다. 저는 미래학자입니다. 저는 경제학자입니다. 혹은 저는 이런이런 일을 합니다. 이런 식으로 자신을 소개합니다. 대부분의 사람은 상사의 지시를 따라야 하는 직장에서 일합니다. 그 대가로 받는 월급을 통해 본인의 가치를 확인합니다. 그런데 직장에서 나와 미지의 영역에서 본인만의 삶을 개척해야 한다고 합시다. 인터넷을 도구로 스스로 외부와 자신을 연결해야 합니다. 이 자리에 많이 와 계신 기업인이라면 이 같이 스스로 결정을 내려야 하는 상황에 익숙하겠지만, 평범한 직장인들에게는 큰 도전입니다. 개인이 도전하는 문화를 활성화하려면 TV나 영화 등을 통해 독립적인 자기 고용자에 대한 긍정적인 이미지를 심어주어야 합니다. 이 같은 홍보 없이 고용형태가 바뀌면, 사람들은 자신이 더 이상 직장인이 아니라는 사실에 자존감과 정체성을 잃어 큰 문제가 될 수 있습니다.

Maslow's Hierarchy of Needs

- **Self-actualization**
  desire to become the most that one can be
- **Esteem**
  respect, self-esteem, status, recognition, strength, freedom
- **Love and belonging**
  friendship, intimacy, family, sense of connection
- **Safety needs**
  personal security, employment, resources, health, property
- **Physiological needs**
  air, water, food, shelter, sleep, clothing, reproduction

매슬로의 욕구단계설은 여러분도 아실 겁니다. 개인의 욕구에 관한 이론입니다. 물리적 욕구, 애정, 소속감, 안정감 등 단계별로 다양한 욕구가 있습니다. 그런데 이를 사회 전체에도 적용할 수 있습니다. 1981년만 하더라도 전세계 인구의 절반 이상이 빈곤층이었습니다. 현재는 이 비율이 10%로 떨어졌습니다. 덕분에 20억명이 가난에서 벗어나며 빈곤과의 전쟁에서는 승리했습니다. 물질적 결핍에서 벗어나면 다음 단계의 욕구를 충족해야 합니다. 그 점에서 한 욕구를 충족하면 보다 상위의 욕구로 올라간다는 매슬로의 이론은 사회 전체에도 유용합니다. 보다 높은 수준의 욕구는 스스로 삶에 대한 결정을 내림으로써 만족할 수 있습니다. 가령 제가 하는 일의 경우 업무, 놀이, 여가가 모두 뒤섞여 있습니다. 그리고 얼만큼 일하거나 쉴지는 상사의 지시 없이 제가 결정합니다.

Scenario 3 Your Personal AI Avatar searches the web while you sleep…

… then wakes you up in the morning ….with all kinds of interesting things to do, some for income, some because the are just fun, and some that are both all with smart contacts if needed.

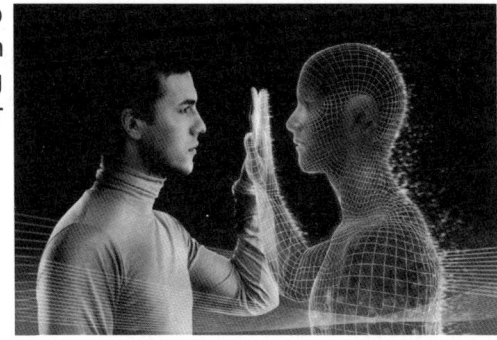

시나리오 3에서는 사람마다 아바타가 있습니다. 이 아바타는 스페인 은행인 BBVA에서 IT를 총괄한 분이 개발했는데, 개인의 투자 전략을 대신 세워주는 아바타입니다. 우리가 자는 동안에 이 아바타는 인터넷을 검색하며 여러 투자 옵션의 수익률을 계산합니다. 그리고 아침에 일어난 고객에게 투자 전략을 제시합니다. 은행들이 왜 이런 아바타를 개발할까요? 고객의 자산이 늘면 은행에게도 이득이기 때문입니다. 그래서 무료 이메일 서비스처럼 아바타도 고객에게 공짜로 제공합니다. 아바타 덕분에 고객은 투자 수익을 창출할 수 있습니다. 아바타는 15개의 유망 투자종목과 15개의 투지 진략을 선정하고, 이를 바탕으로 계약서를 생성합니다. 고객은 투자금이 있다는 사실만 입증하면 됩니다. 덕분에 고객은 손쉽게 수익을 창출할 수 있습니다. 이 세 번째 시나리오가 가장 낙관적인 시나리오입니다.

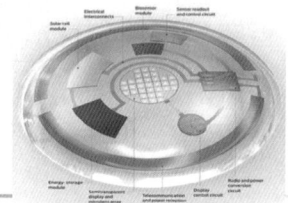

다음으로 증강 지능입니다. 이 두 기업인이 무엇을 발명했는지 아실 겁니다. 이 슬라이드에는 2030-2050년에 수백만명이 증강 지능을 가지게 될 것이라고 적었는데, 이는 보수적으로 잡은 수치입니다. 수백만이 아니라 수십억이 증강 지능을 가진다고 합시다. 2050년의 세계 인구는 90억에서 100억명입니다. 이 중에서 노동인구는 60억명입니다. 그 중에서 절반만 인터넷에 접속해서 증강 지능을 가져도 수십억 명의 천재가 탄생합니다. 여러분이 경영하는 회사에서 모든 직원이 천재라고 생각해 보십시오. 과거와는 다른 직원관리 방식이 필요합니다.

Some examples of 93 actions assessed

- Make increasing intelligence an objective of education.
- In parallel to STEM education create a hybrid system of self-paced inquiry-based learning for self-actualization, creativity, critical thinking, and human relations using new AI tools.
- Create international standards for narrow and general AI with a governance system to enforce them (maybe similar to the International Atomic Energy Agency – IAEA).
- Produce alternative cash flow projections for universal basic income to see if/when it is financially sustainable.
- Put memes in advertisements to help the cultural transition to new forms of economics and work.
- Create personal AI/Avatars able to match peoples' skills and interests with income opportunities worldwide which can make smart contracts to support self-employment.
- Shift education/learning systems more toward mastering skills than mastering a profession.
- Public/private research should explore the cultural transition for a new social contract between the government and the citizens who potentially could be both unemployed and augmented geniuses.
- Art/media/entertainment leaders should engage the public in anticipating cultural changes due to potential impacts of future technologies.

당사에서는 워크샵도 열고, 전문가 의견도 청취하면서 기술의 변화에 맞추어 어떤 행동이 필요한지 종류별로 정리했습니다. 자세한 내용은 보고서에서 읽으실 수 있습니다. 여기 93개의 행동이 필요하다고 슬라이드에 나와 있습니다. 많은 조사와 의견 청취를 바탕으로 정리한 내용입니다. 다만 과학적인 증거보다는 주관적 인식에 근거해서 93개의 필요 행동을 선정했습니다. 여기 몇 가지 예가 나와 있습니다. 하나는 '지능 보강을 교육의 목표로 삼는다'입니다. 뇌의 기능에 대해서는 그간 많은 연구가 이루어졌습니다. 제가 어렸을 적에 비하면 큰 변화입니다. 당시만 하더라도 뇌는 정적인 상태에 있으며, 뉴런이 늘어날 수 없다는 인식이 지배적이었습니다. 그러나 이는 사실이 아니라는 점이 밝혀졌습니다. 평범한 IQ 보유자도 지능을 5-10% 향상시킬 수 있습니다. 체육에서 신체 능력을 향상시키는 것처럼, 인지 교육을 통해 지능을 끌어올릴 수 있습니다.

기존의 이공계 교육과 더불어 학습자 주도와 탐구 중심의 교육을 실시할 수 있습니다. AI를 활용한 교육을 통해 자기 실현을 촉진하고 창의성과 비판적 사고, 대인 능력을 기를 수 있습니다. 저희 보고서에서는 한국과 핀란드의 사례를 들고 있습니다. 한국과 핀란드 학생의 학업 성취도는 비슷하지만 교육 시스템은 완전히 다릅니다. 한국식 교육에서는 최대한 많은 지식을 단기간에 흡수해야 합니다. 반대로 핀란드 교육에서는 창의성 함양에 초점이 맞춰져 있습니다. 초기에는 창의성 중심의 교육을 받은 핀란드 학생이 학업 성취도 점수는 낮지 않을까 하는 우려가 있었습니다. 그런데 뚜껑을 열어 보니 점수도 나쁘지 않았습니다. 보다 유연한 사고능력을 기를수록 지적능력의 향상도 쉽다는 점을 보여주는 사례입니다.

협의의 AI와 범용 AI에 관한 국제적 기준 및 거버넌스를 확립해야 합니다. 그리고 이 기준을 적용하며 지속적으로 개선해야 합니다. 대단히 중요한 부분입니다. 가령 원자력 산업에서 국제원자력 기구(IAEA)가 없었다면 핵무기가 사용되었을지도 모릅니다. 인류 문명이 파멸되었을 수도 있습니다. 그만큼 기준과 거버넌스의 마련이 중요합니다. 협의의 AI와 범용 AI의 발전을 제대로 관리하지 못하면 그 폐해는 핵무기만큼 클 것입니다.

기본소득 도입 시 어떤 현금흐름이 발생할지 시나리오별 전망을 해야 합니다. 제가 처음부터 기본소득에 관심을 갖지는 않았습니다. 그런데 AI가 대량으로 실업자를 양산할 수 있음을 깨달은 후 생각이 달라졌습니다. 직업이 사라지면 기존의 사회 계약이 깨집니다. 학교에서 열심히 공부해서 취직하고 법을 준수하면, 퇴직 후 연금을 수령하고 의료보험 혜택도 받으며 안정된 노후를 누릴 수 있다는 것이 사회 계약의 골자입니다. 그런데 45세에 갑자기 실직한다고 합시다. 그동안 열심히 살아왔고 본인에게는 아무 책임이 없는데도 일자리를 잃은 경우입니다. 제가 시나리오 3에서 기본소득의 가능성에 주목한 것도 이 때문입니다. 인구의 절반이 길거리에 내몰리는 상황을 놔둘 수는 없는 일입니다. 이 같은 가능성을 피하기 위해서라도 여러 정책적 대안을 공유하며 고민해야 합니다.

밈(meme)은 사회적으로 전파되는 아이디어를 뜻합니다. 이 밈을 바꾸는 광고 캠페인을 진행할 수도 있습니다. 노동과 직업에 관한 기존의 인식으로부터 벗어나는 것입니다. 개인별로 맞춤형 AI와 아바타를 생성하여 각자의 능력에 맞는 일자리를 찾도록 지원할 수도 있습니다. 교육의 초점도 직무 중심에서 역량 중심으로 전환되어야 합니다. 물론 직무 능력은 여전히 중요합니다. 그러나 직무는 바뀔 수 있습니다. 여기 변호사 분들도 와 계실 텐데요, 변호사 업무에서 판례 검색과 소장 작성이 높은 비중을 차지합니다. 그리고 이 업무는 상당부분 자동화가 가능합니다.

그러고보니 인공지능을 경영에 어떻게 접목하면 좋을지 질문을 받은 기억이 나는군요. 이에 대한 답을 간단하게 말씀드리겠습니다. 의류든 신문이든 제품의 종류는 상관없습니다. 여러분의 생산 공정에서 단순 반복적인 작업은 무엇인지 목록을 작성하셔야 합니다. 단순 반복적인 작업은 자동화가 가능합니다. 굳이 직접 맡을 필요없이 외주를 주면 됩니다. 그리고 "어떻게 AI를 활용해서 조직을 바꿀 수 있을까요"라고 물어본 분은 거의 없었는데요, 말씀 드렸다시피 여러분의 생산 공정에서 자동화가 가능한

부분부터 적어야 합니다. 절대로 이 작업을 AI 회사에 맡겨서는 안 됩니다. 생산 공정은 외부 업체가 아닌 여러분이 가장 잘 파악하고 있기 때문입니다. 생산 공정의 단계별로 AI 적용이 가능한 부분을 파악하면, 이제 생산현장에 이 기술을 활용할 수 있습니다.

정부와 민간의 연구소는 AI의 등장으로 사회 계약이나 노동에 대한 인식이 어떻게 바뀔지를 중점적으로 봐야 합니다. 더불어 어떤 일자리가 사라질지, 어떻게 노동자의 지능을 증강할 수 있을지를 연구해야 할 것입니다. 시나리오 2에서 대량의 실직자가 발생했는데, 범죄조직이 이들을 조직원으로 고용해서 지능을 증강시키면 해당 조직을 근절하기가 아주 어려워집니다. 제가 슬라이드를 일일이 읽지는 않겠습니다. 관심있으신 분들은 강연이 끝난 후에 배포되는 ppt 슬라이드를 보시면 됩니다. 슬라이드에는 사회의 각 부문별로 맞춤형 대책이 담겨 있습니다. 이공계 교육뿐 아니라 모든 분야에서 기술의 전환에 대비해야 합니다.

ANI – AGI Global Governance

It is argued that creating rules for governance of AI too soon will stifle its development.
Some AGI experts believe it is possible to have AGI as soon as ten years.
Since it is likely to take ten or more years to
- develop ANI to AGI international agreements
- design and international governance system
- begin implementation

Then it is wise to begin exploring governance approaches **now**.

다음으로는 AI 거버넌스입니다. 일각에서는 AI의 거버넌스와 기준을 너무 일찍 마련하면 AI의 발전을 위축시킨다고 주장합니다. 제 생각은 다릅니다. 이 거버넌스와 기준을 마련하는 작업은 10년에서 15년이 걸려도 끝나지 않을 수 있습니다. 가령 미국과 중국이 AI의 기준에 합의한다고 해도, 이 합의가 하루아침에 이루어질 가능성은 낮습니다. 적어도 10년 이상은 걸릴 겁니다. AI 혁신이 위축될까 우려할 필요가 없다는 소리입니다. 일부 전문가들은 범용 AI의 현실화에 10년이 걸릴 것이라 전망합니다. 물론 이 전망이 틀릴 수도 있지만, 통상 군용기술이 민간기술보다 앞서가는 점을 감안할 때 우리 생각보다 일찍 범용 AI가 구현될 수도 있습니다. 반면 AI 거버넌스 기준의 확립은 오랜 시간이 걸리기 때문에 지금부터 그 작업을 시작해야 합니다.

Some initial explorations

University of Oxford's Center for the Governance of AI (cultural issues)
United Arab Emirates Ministry of State for AI
UN Interregional Crime and Justice Research Institute's AI Center
Future of Life Institute (identified 26 nation & 6 international strategies)
Partnership on AI
China AI Industry Alliance
AI for Good Foundation
SingularityNet and Decentralized AI Alliance
Harvard Future Society
United Nations University (common platform for papers on AI governance)

Some Potential Governance Models

1. IAEA-like model or WTO-like with enforcement powers
2. IPCC-like model in concert with international treaties
3. International S&T Organization (ISTO) as an online real-time global collective intelligence system; governance by information power GGCC (Global Governance Coordinating Committees) flexible but enforced by national sanctions, ad hoc legal rulings in different countries, and insurance premiums
4. ISO standards affecting international purchases
5. Put different parts of AGI governance under different bodies like ITU, WTO, WIPO
6. TransInstitution

현재 밀레니엄 프로젝트에서는 이 연구를 진행할지 논의 중입니다. 여러 이해 당사자가 참여 중인데요, 우리가 참조할 수 있는 모델로는 IAEA와 WTO 등이 있습니다. 그 외에도 참고가 될 수 있는 다수의 모델이 있습니다. 각 모델의 분석과 시나리오가 작성되면 그 결과가 공개될 것입니다.

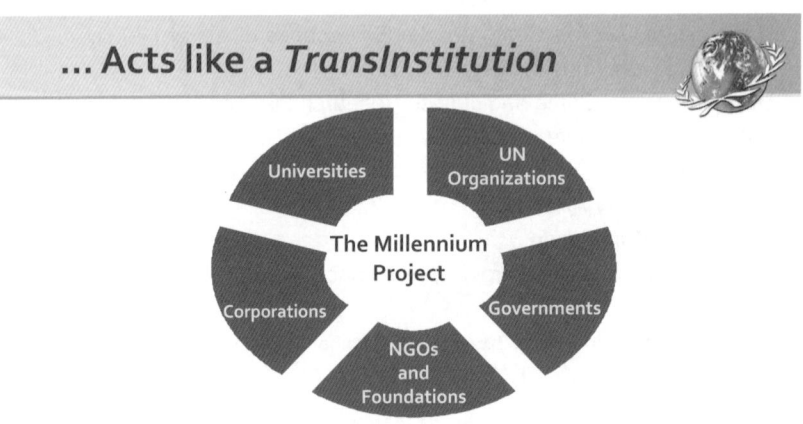

Created in 1996

강연을 마치기 전 밀레니엄 프로젝트에 관해 간단히 언급하고 넘어가겠습니다. 이 프로젝트에 UN의 여러 기구와 정부기관, NGO, 재단, 기업, 대학이 참여했습니다. 그리고 각 당사자는 프로젝트의 인적 구성, 자금 조달, 방향 정립에서 각자의 의견을 제시했습니다. 각 당사자마다 우선 순위에 차이가 있습니다. 기업은 프로젝트의 수익성을 중시합니다. 정부에서는 정치적으로 현실성이 있는지를 따집니다. NGO에서는 프로젝트를 통해 가치를 실현할 수 있는지를 봅니다. UN에서는 국제 협력에 초점을 맞춥니다. UN에서 이 프로젝트를 연구한 적도 있습니다. 그런데 밀레니엄 프로젝트는 통상의 조직과는 달라서 분석에 어려움이 있었습니다. 각 당사자의 장점을 취하는 것이 본 프로젝트의 특징입니다.

Preface
Executive Summary
Ch 1 Global Challenges
Ch 2 2017 State of the Future Index
Ch 3 Future Terrorism & Deterrence
Ch 4 Work/Tech 2050 Scenarios
       and Workshop Strategies
Ch 5 Conclusions
Appendix

현재 밀레니엄 프로젝트에서는 전세계에 65개의 노드를 두고 있습니다. 또한 "세계미래보고서" 시리즈도 발간했습니다. 다시 말씀드리지만 인쇄된 보고서를 구매하실 필요없이 파일을 다운로드 받으시면 됩니다. 본 프로젝트에서는 방법론도 개발하고 있는데, 현재까지 37개의 방법론을 개발했습니다. 그 어떤 기관보다도 많은 숫자입니다. 이 37개 중에서 유일한 정답은 없습니다. 필요에 따라 37개 중에서 적절한 조합을 선택하는 식입니다. 그리고 지금까지 55건의 연구를 수행했는데 슬라이드에 그 목록이 나와 있습니다. 상당히 많은 연구를 했다는 점을 아실 겁니다. 한 연구는 다음 연구의 밑거름이 됩니다. 뇌가 지식을 쌓는 과정과 같습니다. 새로운 정보가 들어오면 기존의 정보와 대조하면서 지식을 개선합니다.

이 슬라이드의 보고서도 다운로드 받으실 수 있습니다. 파키스탄에서 발간된 보고서인데, 인쇄본 입수는 어렵지만 전자파일은 다운로드가 가능합니다. 이 모든 보고서와 연구결과가 집단

지능 시스템의 일부가 됩니다. 오늘 강연장에 많은 분들이 와 주셨는데요, 여러분의 지혜와 경험만 축적해도 집단 지성의 구축에 크게 기여할 수 있을 것입니다. 제 발표는 여기까지입니다. 이제 질문을 받겠습니다. 감사합니다.

인공지능(AI)이 만드는 경제·사회의 미래

질의 응답

Q 유익한 강연 감사드립니다. 소개해주신 시나리오의 결과가 충격적이었는데요. 선생님께서는 역사 문제로 강연을 시작하셨습니다. NT가 일자리를 창출할 것이라고 말씀하셨고요. 이제 신기술의 일자리 창출이 계속 이어지는 단계에 접어들지 않았나 싶습니다. 과거에는 인간이 육체 노동에서 정신 노동으로 전환했습니다. 그런데 이제는 정신 노동, 그러니까 인간의 뇌가 변화의 속도를 따라갈 수 있는지 의문입니다. 60년 전 컴퓨터 프로그램이 처음 등장했을 때만 해도 컴퓨터는 생소한 물건이었습니다. 그런데 이제는 스마트폰 발전 속도조차 따라가기 버거운 세상이 되었습니다.

선생님께서는 지능 향상에 대해 아주 좋은 말씀을 해주셨습니다. 그런데 5-10%의 지능 향상은 암환자에게 반창고나 아스피린을 처방하는 수준에 불과합니다. 실제로 글로벌 리더들의 모습을 보아도 변화에 따라가지 못하는 모습입니다. 기술의 발전에 뒤쳐진 것이죠. 특히 양자 컴퓨터 등의 기술을 보면 인류의 존재 여부조차 의심스러워질 정도입니다. 과연 앞으로도 인류가 존속할 수 있을지, 아니면 이들 기술이 인류의 파멸을 불러올 것인지 알고 싶습니다. 감사합니다.

A 반창고 말씀을 해주셨는데요, 여러분 시력이 0.6이라고 합시다. 이 시력을 안경으로 교정해서 1.0으로 맞춥니다. 만일 시력이 0.4이면 다른 안경으로 시력을 맞추어야 할 것입니다. 제가 드리고 싶은 말씀은 여러분의 지능지수에 상관없이 증강이 가능하다는 것입니다. 제가 언급한 5-10%의 향상은 지능의 일부에 불과합니다. 실제로는 하나가 아닌 10여개의 지능

영역이 존재합니다. 이 복수의 영역을 결합하면 상당한 효과를 거둘 수 있습니다. 지능을 증강해서 천재로 만드는 것도 가능합니다. 물론 지능 증강의 초기에는 부자가 아니면 감당하기 어려울 정도로 비용이 높습니다. 그러나 시간이 지나면서 비용이 낮아지면 기술이 점차 대중화됩니다. 기술의 확산은 추가적인 가격 하락으로 이어지고, 이는 지능 증강의 보급을 한층 더 촉진할 것입니다. 즉 반창고의 자기 증강이 가능해집니다. 아까 발표에서도 하나가 아닌 3개의 시나리오를 소개했습니다. 시간이 남을 때이 3개의 시나리오를 읽어보시기를 권합니다. 질문해주신 문제에 대한 답의 상당수를 시나리오에서 찾을 수 있기 때문입니다.

그런데 말씀해주신 문제를 해결할 수 없다면, 그 논리적인 귀결은 무엇일까요? 사이버 헤로인만 만들어 놓고 손을 놓는 수도 있지만, 그리 바람직한 해결책은 아닙니다. 셰익스피어의 햄릿을 기억하시나요? 작품에는 귀에 독이 부어져 왕이 암살당하는 장면이 있습니다. 만일 우리가 미래 세대에게 포기하라고 계속 얘기하면 나중에는 아예 시도조차 하지 않을 겁니다. 저는 45년 동안 관련 연구를 해 왔습니다. 해답이 없는 문제란 없습니다. 모든 문제에는 답이 있습니다. 아무리 심각한 문제라도 마찬가지입니다. 문제는 리더의 역할입니다. 이 점은 선생님의 질문과도 관련이 있는데, 현재는 제대로 된 리더도 없고 올바른 의사결정 과정도 없습니다. 물론 새로운 유형의 리더십이 등장할 수 없다는 말은 아닙니다. 지뢰금지 조약도 새로운 유형의 리더십 덕분에 체결될 수 있었습니다. 한 시민이 스스로의 노력으로 의미 있는 변화를 이룬 사례입니다. 중요한 것은 믿음입니다. 미국이 철학에서 유일하게 한 기여가 바로 실용주의 철학입니다. 실용주의 철학에 의하면 진실은 알 수 없는 존재입니다. 그러나 실용성 여부는 알 수 있습니다. 만일 무언가가 실용적이면 참입니다. 실용적이지 못하면 거짓입니다. 우리는 비관주의를 경계해야 합니다. 부정적인 측면의 고려는 필요하지만, 이것이 비관주의로 이어져서는 안 됩니다. 밀레니엄 프로젝트에서는 지난 20년간 인류 문명의 미래를 예측하기 위한 지표를 연구했습니다. 20년이나 계속된 연구입니다. 그 점에서 밀레니엄 프로젝트는 패배가 아닌 승리라고 할 수 있습니다. 비관주의에 빠져서는 안 됩니다. 다만 말씀하신대로 실패한 점이 있다면 이를 심각하게 받아들여야 합니다. 즉 비관주의도 곤란하지만, 문제가 없다는 식의 낙관주의도 위험합니다. 객관적 시각과 실용주의, 문제의식을 가진 이상주의야말로 우리가 지향해야 할 상입니다.

 유익하고 많은 문제제기를 한 강연 감사합니다. 이 문제를 하나의 맥락에서 바라보면 어떨까 싶습니다. 선생님께서는 이 분야에 오랫동안 종사해 오셨습니다. 우리가 45세에 실직자가 될 수 있다는 말씀도 하셨고, 밀레니엄 프로젝트가 20년 넘게 연구를 진행 중이라는 말씀도 하셨습니다. 그렇다면 현재 시점에서 봤을 때, 선생님의 시나리오는 얼마나 정확했나요'? 몇 십년이면 시나리오나 방법론의 타당성을 검증하기에는 충분한 시간이라고 생각됩니다. 선생님께서는 본인의 전망이 얼마나 정확하다고 생각하고 계신지 궁금합니다.

A 한 때 핵전쟁이 인류를 파멸시킬 수 있다는 전망이 있었습니다. 이러한 예측이 맞기를 바라는 이는 아무도

없을 것입니다. 그 외에도 현실화되어서는 안 되는 시나리오나 전망이 있습니다. 한 예가 기후 변화입니다. 그 누구도 대기 중 온실가스 농도가 증가하기를 바라지는 않을 것입니다. 최악의 온난화 시나리오가 현실이 되면 인류 문명이 종말을 맞이할 수도 있습니다. 그러나 한편으로는 이 같은 시나리오가 우리에게 경종을 울리는 역할도 합니다. 중요한 것은 예측의 정확성이 아니라 유용성입니다. 경고의 유용성은 분명합니다. 그리고 제 경고를 많은 이들이 심각하게 받아들였습니다. 제가 30년 전에 어떤 전망을 했는지 알고 싶다면, 제가 당시에 쓴 "미래의 마인드(Future Mind)"라는 책을 읽어보시면 됩니다. 당시 저는 '지식의 나무'라는 개념을 언급했습니다. 이 지식의 나무가 바로 현재의 스마트폰입니다. 그리고 국방에 관한 장에서는 미래에 정보전이 일어날 것이라고 썼습니다. 비록 30년 전의 글이지만, 읽어 보시면 현재의 미국과 러시아 정보전을 그대로 묘사하는 것처럼 느껴질 겁니다. 차라리 당시의 제 전망이 빗나가는 편이 나았을 텐데 말이죠. 제가 강연에서 농담삼아 미래를 걸고 내기를 한다고 말씀드렸는데요, 미래에 내기를 건다고 해도 'X가 일어날 것이다'고 전망하면 곤란합니다. '이러이러한 조치를 취하지 않으면 X가 일어날 것이며, 반대의 경우에는 Y가 일어날 것이다'고 해야 맞습니다. 즉 중요한 것은 전망의 정확성이 아닌 유용성입니다. 그렇다면 제 예측이 얼마나 유용한지가 문제되는데요, 그 점은 제가 다음에도 이 자리에 초청받아 강연을 하는지를 보시면 될 것 같습니다.

Q 오늘 강연의 참석자를 위한 질문을 드려도 될까요? 저명한 미래학자로서 한국의 미래를 어떻게 전망하십니까? 2050년이 되면 한국이 지금보다 나아질까요? 제가 생각해도 상당히 까다로운 질문 같습니다.

A 까다로운 질문이어도 괜찮습니다. 아까 말씀드린 이집트의 사례와도 관련이 있는 질문인데요. 먼저 한국이 자국에 대한 경고의 시나리오를 얼마나 진지하게 받아들이는지가 중요합니다. 경고에 어떻게 대응할지는 한국이 결정할 문제입니다. 그러나 경고의 심각성은 인식해야 합니다. 제가 아까 북한 아동의 영양 실조의 현실과 증강 지능의 가능성을 언급했습니다. 구체적인 수치까지는 말씀드리지 않겠지만, 상당수 북한 아동은 정신적 발달이 지체되었습니다. 북한 주민이 유전적으로 문제가 있어서가 아니라, 기아 때문입니다. 북한 주민도 같은 한민족입니다. 그만큼 유전적으로 지적 능력이 우수합니다. 단지 제대로 먹지 못한 결과 뇌가 제대로 발달하지 못했습니다. 만일 한국이 이 문제에 대한 사전 대책을 마련하지 않는다면, 독일보다 더 큰 통일 비용을 짊어지게 될 것입니다. 한국은 특수한 상황에 둘러싸여 있습니다. 주변국인 일본, 중국, 북한 때문에 한국은 항상 외부 위협에 노출되어 있습니다. 다른 지역과 멀리 떨어져 태평양 한복판에 위치하고, 날씨까지 온난한 하와이와는 다릅니다. 한반도는 두 발 뻗고 잘 수 있는 상황이 아니기 때문에 항상 주변 상황에 촉각을 곤두세워야 합니다. 그만큼 한국이이 다른 민족보다 머리를 많이 써야 했습니다.

두 번째로 한국은 빠른 변화를 경험했습니다. 그래서 한국인은 빠른 변화에 익숙합니다. 어찌 보면 한국인의 문화라고도 할 수 있습니다. 그래서인지 한국은 미래의 모습에 관심이 많습니다. 제가 한국에 처음에 왔을 때 버스를 타고 신라 호텔로 이동했는데, 이동하면서 5개의 호텔 정류장을 거쳤습니다. 한 정류장에서는 SBS 방송 기자와 함께 "이동통신이 미래" 비슷한 제목이 적힌 현수막이 보였습니다. 그 다음 정류장의 호텔에서도 "XX의 미래"류의 행사가 열리고 있었습니다. 나머지 정류장의 호텔들도 마찬가지였습니다. 어찌된 일인지 의아할 정도였습니다. 제가 말을 지어내고 있다고 생각하신다면 거짓말 탐지기를 쓰셔도 좋습니다.

비화를 하나 들려 드리겠습니다. 박정희 대통령은 초등학교 교사 출신입니다. 역사상 가장 놀라온 경제 발전을 이끌어낸 지도자이기도 합니다. 상당히 드문 성공사례라고 할 수 있습니다. 당시 냉전이 한창이었던 당시 헤르만 칸(Herman Kahn)이라는 미래학자가 있었습니다. 칸은 당대 최고의 미래학자로서 여러 시나리오를 썼는데, 박정희 대통령도 자주 만났습니다. 정말인지 의심스러우면 직접 확인하셔도 좋습니다. 이 강연이 녹화되는 것 맞죠? 제가 혹시 실언이라도 했는지 걱정되는군요.

박정희 대통령을 비판적으로 보는 사람은 그의 업적을 인정하려 들지 않을 겁니다. 반대로 박정희 대통령을 긍정적으로 보는 사람은 그가 미국의 미래학자 영향을 받았다는 사실을 받아들이려 하지 않을 겁니다. 미래학자가 왜 필요한지 의구심을 표하는 이도 있는데, 이 일화야말로 미래학자의 가치를 잘 보여준다고 할 수 있습니다. 그럼에도 오늘 전까지는 이 스토리를 한 번도 들지 못하셨을 겁니다. 아마도 관심을 가지지 않았기 때문입니다. 비록 출판은 되지 않았지만, 한국에서 관련 책까지 저술되었는데도 그렇습니다.

한국인들은 저 같이 터무니없는 얘기를 하는 미래학자에 관심이 많은 것 같습니다. 적어도 저를 이 자리에 초대해주신 것을 보면 말이죠. 제가 여기서 강연을 하고 싶다고 요청한 것이 아니라, 세계경제연구원에서 먼저 저에게 문의를 했거든요. 저는 오늘 전까지는 이 연구원이 어떤 기관인지도 몰랐습니다. 그러나 한국인이 열린 마인드를 갖고 있음은 분명하며, 이는 큰 자산이 될 겁니다. 지나친 비관주의에 빠지지 않는다는 전제 하에서요. 물론 비관주의가 무용하다는 말은 아닙니다. 낙관적인 전망은 비관적 시나리오의 검증을 먼저 거쳐야 하기 때문입니다. 그러나 식사에 비유하면 비관주의는 요리가 아니라 양념이라고 할 수 있습니다.

저는 한국의 앞날이 밝다고 생각합니다. 한국인은 과거의 성공을 통해 이미 그 저력을 입증했습니다. 이 같은 성공은 가나와 비교하면 더욱 두드러집니다. 전세계적으로도 자주 언급되는 사례입니다. 그러나 이제는 한국이 경제 패러다임의 전환을 이룩해야 할 때입니다. 한국은 지금까지 추격형 경제로서 성공을 거두었습니다. 선진국의 성공을 모방해서 경제 성장을 이룩하는 전략이었습니다. 모든 분야에서 선진국을 따라잡은 것은 아니지만, 이제는 더 이상 한국이 추격형 경제가 아니라고 말할 수 있을 정도로 성장했습니다. 이제는 한국이 경제 대국과 어깨를 나란히 하고 있습니다. 물론 중국 등에 비하면 경제 규모는 작지만, 인공지능 등의 지식 산업에서 선진국 못지 않은 경쟁력을 갖추었습니다. 한국은 역사와 지정학적 입지를 바탕으로 지금의 위치에 섰습니다. 저는 앞으로도 한국이 계속 발전하기를 바랍니다. 단, 스스로를 비관주의에 가두는 것은 피해야 합니다.

Jerome C. Glenn

Jerome C. Glenn, an internationally renowned futurist, is CEO of The Millennium Project and lead-author of the State of the Future reports for the past twenty years. He has over 40 years of Futures Research experience working for governments, international organizations, and private industry in the area of Science & Technology Policy, Environmental Security, and Economics. His recent research includes 'Work/Technology 2050: Scenarios and Actions' and 'Future Elements of the Next Global Economy.'

Artificial Intelligence (AI) and its Impact on the Future of Economy and Society

Jerome C. Glenn
Futurist
CEO of The Millennium Project

First thing, what we've got to remember about technology is we are supposed to be in charge of it rather than it in charge of us.

Let's start with basic things that I think we all agree on. When people talk about AI and its effect on a society, people say, "Well, everytime there's a big transition, going from agricultural age to industrial age is going to get rid of jobs, and going from industrial age to information and knowledge age kind of lose jobs. What's different this time? Why wouldn't it be exactly the same?" So what's different?

Each economic transition created more jobs than those lost

Why is it different this time?
1. the acceleration of technological change
2. the globalization, interactions, and synergies among NTs
3. the existence of a global platform—the Internet—for simultaneous technology transfer ... with far fewer errors in the transfer than in the past
4. standardization of data bases and protocols
5. few plateaus or pauses of change allowing time for individuals and cultures to adjust to the changes
6. billions of empowered people in relatively democratic free markets able to initiate activities
7. machines can learn how you do what you do, and then do it better than you.

This time, one, the acceleration of change. I think everybody agrees that changes are made a lot faster. Consider life of your grandparents compared to yours. That's extraordinary amount of change. Even your parents' compared to yours. A lot of changes. Who would have believed 30 years ago, that you would outproduce the United States in steel, communications technology, etc., etc., etc.? Acceleration of change in the course the fast you go with new technology, the fast you're able to go, so as the acceleration of the acceleration. That's new.

Globalization, interaction and synergies among NTs. NT is a simple phrase meaning "next technology," just like we have ICT that takes into account packet switching, data cable, software. We put them all together and say ICT because we don't want to keep repeating ourselves. We don't have to say nano-technology, cognitive science, synthetic biology. It's just too much so we say NT. The NTs will have synergies among them, look at how many different technologies are integrated into your cell phone. That's new. You can say "There was a globalization 50 years ago." Yes. Not compared to today.

Three. Existence of global platform, the Internet. This means we can transfer knowledge simultaneously and without error. In the 1980s, I was helping to put around the world, in the third world mostly, what were called packet switching. That's what makes Internet cheap. You make a packet out of your data and you switch it to a satellite. Packet switching.

Suppose I had to get in an airplane, get out of an airport, talk to somebody, maybe decision happens, and then get somewhere else. That takes years. Do you know when the internet protocol was created? 50 years ago. It's 50th anniversary of the Internet Protocol. 1968-69. When did we start to use it for real? 1990. It took a long time. Now we have the platform – we didn't have it before – and that changes things very fast and without errors. I might forget something when I talk to somebody when I get out of the airplane. But now, you hit a button and the whole world gets it. Simultaneously. Software. Data. That's extraordinary.

Imagine that one of you gets a new insight. Simultaneously you all get the same insight. Of course, if we create a collective intelligence system for your organization, maybe you can do that. We don't have that on the databases but we now have a software. That's new.

Standardization of databases and protocols. When I was in the United Nations University Liaison between Tokyo and Washington, one of the things we did, we had standards for answering the question what would people eat today. Sounds sort of dumb and simple but by having the standards across the whole world, you can actually do research and learn and learn and learn. We didn't have that when we went from the industrial age to the information age.

Five. Few plateaus for pauses. This is really important but hard to communicate. My first laptop was 1992. I now have a laptop. I granted. It's more powerful and all that. But it still is a laptop. So I had a chance to adjust to it. It didn't keep changing all over the place. You all are using laptops, today they look a little bit similar to laptops a long time ago. But if you have AI pushing all of these things together, you don't have a same chance to adjust and get used to it. We accept the idea of a laptop computer. But what happens in 1992, something else came out for contact lenses. You wouldn't have a chance to get used to it. Now you're in contact lenses, now you're in implant. You know, it's just too much. If we go into this direction, then people think it'll be difficult for society to adjust to the changes because of the speed. That's also new.

Six. Billions – not millions – billions of empowered people in relatively democratic free markets able to initiate activities. Go back to your grandparents, or even your parents. What was the idea? It's a catch-up economy. We're going to follow if this is the way to do it. Well, now, much of the world is on even playing field. The questions we'll talk about today are also being talked about in Silicon Valley together. There's no catch-up coming up. We're inventing together. You can connect half of the world to the other half of the world through the Internet. We didn't have this ability before.

People can initiate things. I don't know if you know the story about the landmine treaty. A woman in Maine didn't like the idea that children are being blown up by landmines around the world. It's not just demilitarize, all around the world, tons of them around the world. So she initiated the conversation on the internet which led to an international treaty. She, acting alone, initiated an important thing for the world. More and more people would be able to do that. That's new. In the past, we said "You're the boss. End of conversation. What's to think?"

The last one is that machine can learn how you do, what you do, and then do better than you do. These are seven reasons. I stress this to begin with because I am very tired of hearing people say "There's nothing new under the sun. We're going to create more jobs. Don't worry." These are seven reasons saying that's not true. So if you forget everything I say, you can now go to sleep. Remember these seven points.

Inevitability of New Economics, Changing social contract and human rights

- Concentration of wealth is increasing
- Income gaps are widening
- Employmentless economic growth seems the new norm
- Return on Investment in capital and technology is usually better than labor
- Future technologies can replace much of human labor
- Long-term structural unemployment is a "business as usual" or "surprise free" trend forecast
- **What can we do about this?**

Inevitability of new economics, changing social contract with human beings. We know the concentration of wealth is increasing. It doesn't seem to matter where you are. It doesn't seem to matter whether you're in socialist system or capitalist system. It seems to be species phenomena. Income gaps are widening. "Employmentless" economic growth is the new norm. Return on investment in capital and technology is usually better than on labor. Future technologies can replace much of human labor, mental and physical. Long-term structural unemployment is a "business as usual," "surprise-free" forecast.

Future Work/Technology 2050 Study

1. Literature and Related Research Review
2. Real-Time Delphi on questions not asked or poorly answered
3. Three Global Scenario Drafts to 2050
4. Three Separate RTDelphi's for Feedback on each Scenario
5. Final Scenarios, given for Millennium Project Nodes
6. National Workshops to Explore Long-range Strategies
7. Collect suggestions from the national planning workshops, distilled in to 93 actions, assess all via five (5) Real-Time Delphi's
8. Final Report for Public Discussion

If you had over half of the world unemployed, that's social chaos. That's a surprise-free forecast. So what do we do about this? The first thing we did is we read everybody else's work. Normal sort of thing. We read a research. I'll give you a little feedback on that. One. Not one of the 30-50 studies I read mentions synthetic biology once. Synthetic biology is not gene editing. Gene editing is you take a species' gene, DNA, you knock something out, you put something else in or knock it out and leave it that way, but it's still a human or still a rose or still a turkey.

Synthetic biology is not that. You stand in front of a computer screen, or sit, and you put together what are the capabilities you want a new kind of species to do. Clean the plaque in your brain, dust the floor, what do you want it to do? And you put together genetic material from completely different species electronically on a screen first. Then you test it out, is it going to be coherent, then you buy those biological products. One of the biggest suppliers is in Hong Kong, GenScript, and yes I do own stock in GenScript. You can now buy these parts and you can make species from scratch. Think of everything nature does and you can't do. That's a big business opportunity.

Or take the first one about the brain. If you can make an organism, a micro-organism, to go into brain and clean out the plaque in the brain, that means when you're 99 years old, your brain can be as fresh as when you were 25. Now, you've got an aging population. This is serious. You know the financial projections on this. So if all these people are sick and getting retired, it is going to kill your economy. You know this. It's a matter of time. But, if they're alive and intelligent and connected to the Internet, making a living, they're paying taxes. They're financial assets, not financial liabilities. And the cascading effect from the brain to the rest of the body has a lot to do with things put you into hospital, not everything but lot. That one thing is a very big deal. Or you can make one that picks up the dust. You have a pile of these things, you put them into a corner and at the end of the conference, these things are rolling out all night long, picking up the dust, like hours, slow motion, and the next morning there's a pile of dirt on the other side. No vacuum cleaner. No vacuum cleaner salesman. No electricity. No trash to pick – you know there's still trash but not as the same way because then you can put this into some compost pile probably.

Anyways, stress this to say, synthetic biology maybe a bigger deal than in the industrial evolution and these 30 or 50 study totally missed that. Very important. We spent some time studying synthetic biology. Tremendous economic potential is here. This is where a lot of economic growth and jobs actually come from.

We did a survey that has questions that we thought from our first step were either not asked, like synthetic biology, or badly answered. For example, a lot of the studies said "We're going to solve this problem with STEM (Science, Technology, Mathematics, and Engineering) education." What percent of workforce of 6 billion people can really make a living in science, technology, and engineering? Not everybody and probably a minority. What about the rest of the people? So we put together this questionnaire, we gave it to our 65 nodes around the world, they identify who should they ask the questions, because I won't know who in Iran knows the most.

Iran will know. Then we took all the information together and we wrote three draft scenarios. Then we took those three draft scenarios and we sent three separate questionnaires back out, and had them criticized so that they would be more plausible.

Quick pause on scenarios. The way scenario planning is done today is sort of okay. Better than nothing. But that's not the purpose of scenarios to see what's robust in four different views of the future. Purpose of scenarios is to find out what you didn't know that you should have known, but you didn't know enough to even know that. They were created at the RAND Corporation to figure out how to prevent World War III, because in the past, military historians could tell you all kinds of things but they were in different analyses. It was like a thermonuclear war which ends the game. So much of the "if-then" reasoning, the risk analysis, all that you had to throw out of the door. Start from scratch, so they wrote stories to find out what they didn't know. That was the purpose of scenarios. What you see in these two uncertainties, you make a little grid, to see in this scenario, this, and in this scenario, this? No. How did that scenario write there? What are the cause and effect links? It exposes what you don't know. That's the important part. Don't contract out scenario writing to some science fiction writer because he learns and you don't. Your inside staffs should write the scenarios, and it's very important for them to get to points that says "I have no idea."

One of these scenarios, Scenario 3 had some guaranteed income, so I said "Okay, what's the financial sustainability?" I wanted to do a cash flow projection. Cash flow projection, a reasonable business tool. Nobody had one. When I started writing, I didn't know that nobody knew what they were talking about. It's a hard statement, I know, but if you do business, you should do a cash flow projection. It's a normal thing to do. I talked to the Swiss. I talked to the Finnish. All these people doing these guaranteed income projections in studies, they didn't have cash flow projection. So we had to integrate that as well.

We gave these scenarios to these nodes around the world and said "Alright, I want you to bring together." The idea is that you read the scenarios to open up the mined possibilities. We don't know the truth of the future. Futurists, serious futurists, don't claim to know the truth of the future. A flying saucer could come over Seoul and everything gets changed. But what we do know is, we know about possibilities. That's why we do alternative scenarios to make the point that I'm not saying X is the truth. I want you to think about it. These are possibilities, so what are you going to do today? Then we did this workshops, after we read the scenarios, we throw them out and just say what do we do as a country. So we did a bunch of countries and a lot of actions came out of that. That's in that little hand-out, it was in the front available.

Three Forms of Artificial Intelligence

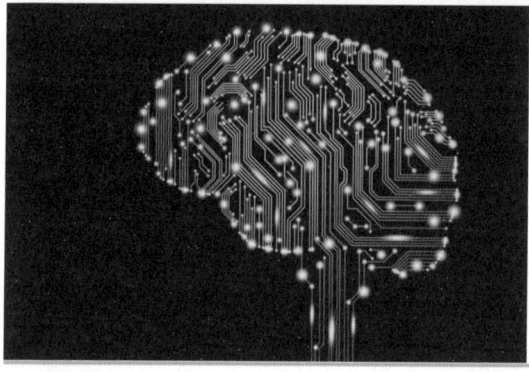

- Artificial Narrow Intelligence
- Artificial General Intelligence
- Artificial Super Intelligence

Now, AI. There are three kinds of artificial intelligence. It gets confused and I am very upset with this confusion because it's hurting decision making. When people say AI, you should ask "Are you talking about narrow AI? Are you talking about general AI? Are you talking about super AI?" We're talking before about Alpha-Go. A lot of people in Korea got nervous and went "Oh my god, this artificial intelligence is here today."

Narrow is here today. It's not a science fiction. AI that drives a car cannot diagnose cancer. But if we get to general intelligence – which we may never get to by the way, it's not a guarantee – it's very, very, very tough. So we may never have it. But if I take a bet, I'll take it a bet, futures do make the best. What futurists don't say is it's going to happen for sure. To be an honorable man, I had to say it might not happen. But it might happen. It's possible even in 10-15 years.

Artificial general intelligence can drive your car, diagnose cancer, make appointments, do all kinds of things, and share and draw on artificial narrow intelligences around the world, the Internet of Things (IoT) around the world, anything. It could make artificial telephone calls to ask your opinion just like when you're given a noble problem. You ask opinions from people, you read articles, you do all kinds of stuffs. That's what artificial general intelligence is designed to do, and it can share simultaneously on a common platform. The advances in one city can be simultaneous with the rest of the city so the growth of the intelligence gets phenomenal with this. So when people talk about, doing a lot of STEM education, that's good under narrow intelligence. Good idea. But if by 2030-2035 we get general, forget it all. We can outthink a dog. It's that kind of distinction we're talking about. The distinction between narrow and general is totally like saying the Internet and a fax machine are tools of the information age. True. But the fax machine and the Internet are really different. That's the kind of confusion happening in the world today. We're confusing these two things all the time.

When Putin says whoever runs AI runs the world, that doesn't mean narrow. He may not know it, but he means general. And when China says we're going to do it in 2030, it may not be clear but probably is talking about general here. That's the big deal.

Super intelligence is defined super as super intelligence sets its own goals, independent of your understanding. That's what science fiction is writing about. That's what Elon Musk is warning about. That's why we're all nervous. If general isn't going to be around a while and super's after that, why are you panicking now? Here's why. We don't know how long it will take to go from general to super. It could be the next moment. It could be never. By definition, we won't know. Now, as a friendly neighborhood futurist who takes bets, I'll take a bet that super intelligence does happen, but I won't take a bet on how long. So we have to get our standards right before we go into general because if we hit general without agreements and standards and good initial conditions, then we lose control. That's where these guys are panicking now because it's going to take us a long time to get all these together, so we've got to start now.

Next Technologies (NT): Imagine How NT Synergies Will Create New Businesses

Artificial Intelligence	Tele-Presence, Holographic Communications
Robotics	
Synthetic Biology & Genomics	Intelligence augmentation
Computational Science	Collective Intelligence
Cloud & Big Data Analytics	Blockchain
Artificial & Augmented Reality	3D/4D Printing Materials/Biology
Nanotechnology (two kinds)	Drones, Driverless Cars (and other autonomous vehicles)
IoT, Tele-Everything & Tele-Everybody, the Semantic Web	Conscious-Technology
Quantum computing	<u>Synergies Among These</u>

Now the reason we say NTs are the technologies that are coming up, each one of them by themselves is a very big deal. I mention synthetic biology in genomics, computational science is where you do simulations instead of a laboratory which means the speed of scientific break-throughs will accelerate. Cloud computing data and analytics, I think you all know about this for predictive analytics, that's pretty well understood in the world. Nano-technology, there's two kinds. What we have today is big machines making little things. That's the nano-tech we have today. The big deal is not that. Big deal is can we make little things make little bigger things making little bigger things like nature. A leaf of a plant is atomically precise manufacturing. It can separate hydrogen and oxygen without heat. We don't know how to do that. We will learn hopefully how to do nano-technology in small stuff going up to big stuff. We do that, that's a giant thing even beyond artificial intelligence as well. IoT, Tele-Everything, Tele-Everybody, semantic web, quantum computing.

How many of you know that you can get free access to quantum computer today? Okay, now you know it. It's small time, it's only about 5 qubits. You can't do much with that. But it is a quantum computer and you can get access from IBM. Can I just get D-Wave? They'll sell you, big price though, a quantum computer. Some people argue whether it is or not but quantum computing is now no longer just a futurists' projection. It's in the early stages. The reason that's such a big deal, explaining this is too hard, everybody knows explaining quantum computing is impossible. I mean it's quantum mechanics. To make a long story short, quantum computing can do things real fast which means the idea of encryption is dead unless you get your own quantum computing. There's a lot of big implications to this, but it's going to take couple of years for us to get there, but each one of these is big deal.

Tele-presence, holographic communications, intelligence augmentation, collective intelligence, blockchain, 3D/4D printing, drones, driverless cars, other autonomous vehicles, conscious-technology, and the synergies among all these things, that's the big thing. That's what NT is. Just like ICT is a synergy among all these software and hardware. Same idea. So we're going to start thinking like this, but the trouble is people say "Well, it's just about AI." It's not just about AI. It's about all these technologies, and it's about the synergies among these.

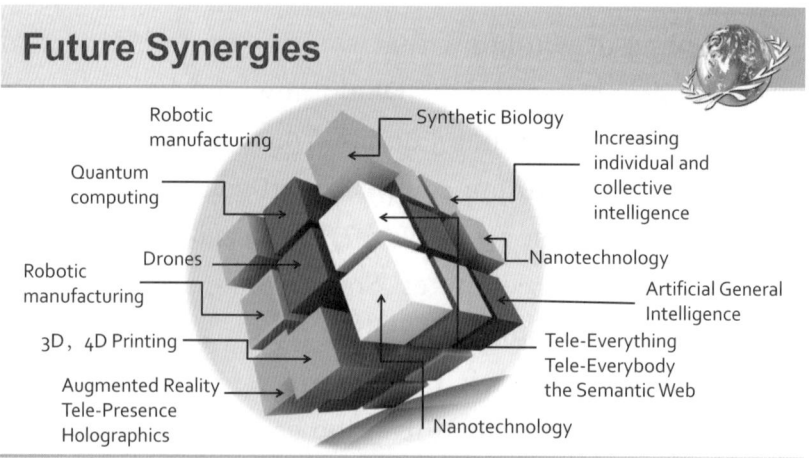

Future Synergies

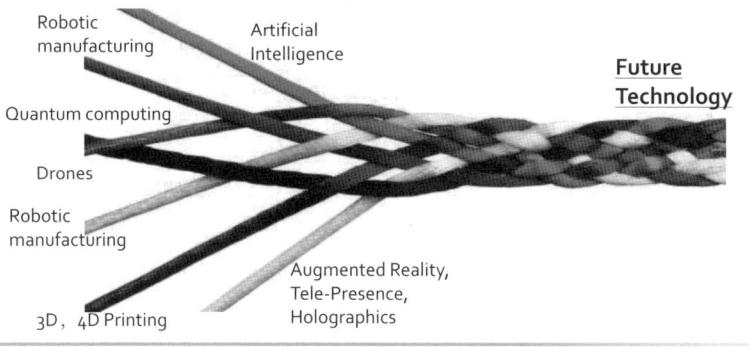

I understand there are few economists in this room, right? My understanding is you make wealth by putting things together that hadn't been put together, that people want. We're in an accelerated process of doing that now. This is the old way of looking a technology. As if they're separate phenomena. That's misleading. When somebody says they were surprised, what does it mean? It means they didn't turn their head and see the other side. They didn't look around. What's happening is this. Integration of technologies. Synergies of them. Think of a puzzle cube where you put things together, and I guarantee, if you like, try this. You'll come up with new ideas. It's almost impossible not to come up with new ideas. What's the implications of nano-technology for synthetic biology? You've never had that question, right? But there are implications. We just haven't thought them through yet or you can braid them together.

Work/Tech Global Scenarios 2050

Each scenario is about 10 pages of detailed cause & effect sequences that illustrate decisions

1. It's Complicated - A Mixed Bag

2. Political/Economic Turmoil – Future Despair

3. If Humans Were Free – The Self-Actualizing Economy

Okay, so we've put all these together into three scenarios just to open up the conversation. The scenario is in the material distributed but you will need to buy them later on. By the way, don't get the hard copy, get the electronic version because the keyword search is a better deal and we don't have to mail it. Go electronic. Anyway, each scenario is about 10 pages, and you can see "if-then"s, how do these things evolve, and I went along like if I don't know about this thing, stop writing, find out.

The first one is "It's Complicated – A Mixed Bag." Now, the reason we went out to 2050, is because we studied other people's studies, they all tended to go five years, maybe 10 years the most. Mostly 5 years. We can't talk about cultural change much in 5 years. We can't talk about economic system changes much in 5 years. But you take all those technologies together and that's going to be a big impact on culture, on economics. So we figured let's go out to 2050 to give us enough elbow room to actually think and therefore have early warnings, because some of these will take years to address. We've got to start thinking about them. But there are still a lot of changes in that because if the acceleration of change is accelerating, that means by 2050, it's quite different than now. There's still business as usual and trend forecast.

The second one is "Political/Economic Turmoil – Future Despair," I'll talk about each of these a little bit later, and the third one is "everything works." So if you got a friend who's too pessimistic, have them read Scenario 3. If you got a friend who's just too optimistic, have them read Scenario 2. That will sober them up real fast. Scenario 2 is a very rough scenario. But all of these are plausible. I mean, we had discussions about this all around the world, so I don't mean that they're going to happen but they're plausible.

Global Employment Assumptions
Workforce 3 billion 2000; 6 billion 2050

	Scenario 1 Business as Usual	Scenario 2 Political Turmoil	Scenario 3 Self-Actualization
Employed	2 Billion	1 Billion	1 Billion
Self-Employed	2 Billion	1 Billion	3 Billion
Unemployed or in transition	1 Billion	2 Billion	1 Billion
Informal Economy	1 Billion	2 Billion	1 Billion

These are just assumptions. Don't take this like an economic forecast. These are just assumptions just to give you a sense of the distinctions. In Scenario 1, business as usual we figure, we still have 2 billion people more or less, employed in a normal way we talk about employment. You have a boss, you have income and so forth. Self-employment about 2 billion as you know the trend of the area because remember we do trend forecast. If the trend's going up, that means by 2050, you got a lot more people self-employed. So that's about 2 billion. Unemployed or in transition, about a billion. And the informal economy, about a billion. As you know it's really tough to change the informal economy. Something like, what, 60% of Egypt? Weren't there an Egyptian Ambassador here by the way? Good. Thank you. 60% I understand your country's informal economy. (Impossible to know.) See? That's what I'm saying. We don't know. But a good guess. It's a lot of people. To change that in Egypt, it's very, very, very difficult. So even out to 2050, but around the world not just Egypt, so we're trying to be plausible. But even in Scenario 3 this looking good, we still figure about a billion people in the best case scenario in the informal economy. This simply means, there're still economic activities, but they're just not paying taxes or not registered. In Scenario 2, you got a billion people working, self-employment about a billion, unemployed 2 billion, and informal about 2 billion. Now, if the workforce in the year 2000 was about 3 billion, and if the workforce in 2050 is about 6 billion, not the population, just the workforce, then that means in Scenario 1, you do have more jobs because you have 2 billion here and 2 billion here. That's 4 billion. Alright? Scenario 3 you got 4 billion as well. It's just different mix. Scenario 2 you only got 2 billion. So Scenario 2 is the one we figure you actually end up with fewer jobs.

Scenario 1:
It's Complicated – A Mixed Bag

- A business-as-usual trend projection
- Increasing acceleration of change with both intelligence and stupidity
- Irregular adoption of advance technology
- Major employment growth in Biotech Industries
- High unemployment where governments did not create long-range strategies
- Mixed success on the use of universal basic income.
- Giant corporations grow beyond government control, in this government-corporate, virtual-3D, multi-polar world of 2050.

The first one, business as usual trend projection is increasing acceleration of change in both intelligence and stupidity. Because that's the truth. We have intelligent decision and we have stupid decisions. Right? So part of the trend, you still have stupidity and you still have intelligence going on. Irregular adoption of advanced technology, major employment growth, mostly in biotech industries, high unemployment rate where governments did not create long-term strategies. I don't know if you know this, but a lot of people, World Bank makes this comment, they say 30-40 years ago that basics of Ghana and Korea were about the same. Korea obviously did a different job. You had some long-term planning. Long-term thinking here. Ghana did not have that. Mixed success in universal basic income. Giant corporations grow beyond government control, and in this government corporate, virtual-3D, multi-polar world of 2050.

Imagine that you got hands-free, phones-free, laptop-free AI symbiosis with contact lenses and all kinds of other things that these are actually being 3D printed today. Experimental. You've got some here in Korea already where you can do, I forgot the name, but one of the Korean corporations already has contact lenses being experimented where you can click and make photographs and send it off through the Internet. But you'll end up with distinctions between virtual reality (VR) and physical reality, and who cares. Like in the early days of e-mail, you could make a distinction between a telephone and a computer but you couldn't separate them.

In the same way, all gets mixed together, no one would, like if this is 2050, whether I'm an android or whether I'm a hologram or whether I'm a flash, you don't care. The distinction, it will just be totally buried in this sort of the world.

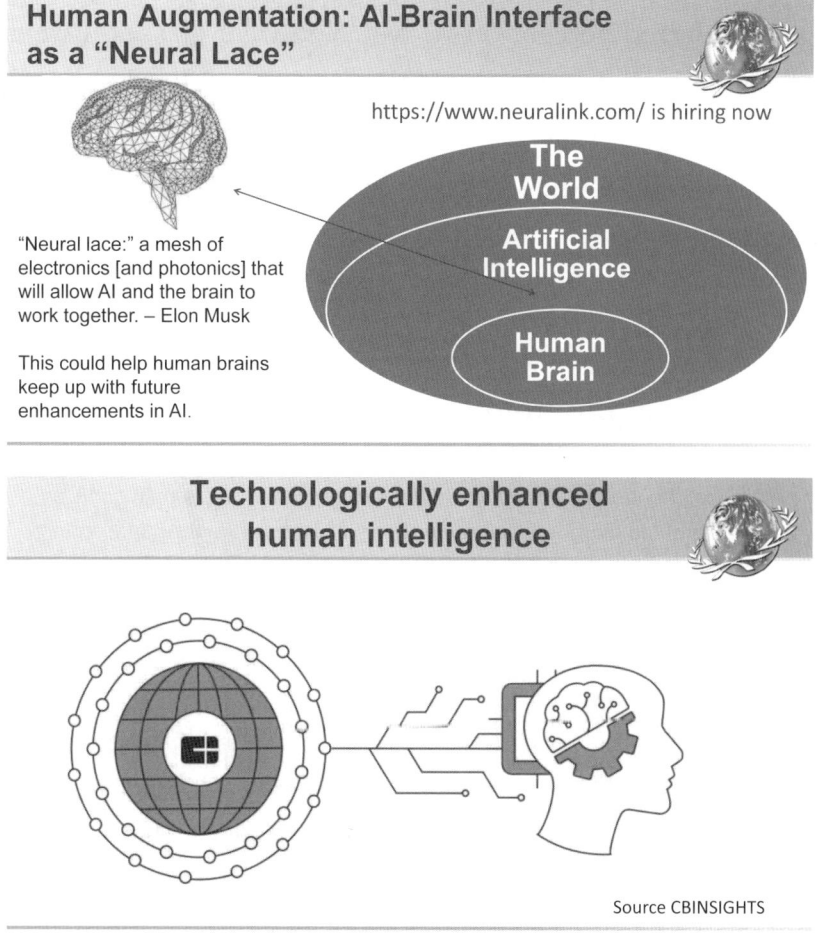

Right now, as you know Elon Musk, he's got fibers before

even tested and robotically implanted into brain that are something like 50 times smaller diameter than hair. So this is not just a speculation. We may be able to connect the human mind to the internet and that's a trend forecast. Which means if you take an IQ test, and you got pattern recognition software, read the IQ test questions, you should be able to get a hundred percent on IQ test. You wear glasses, I wear glasses. We all pass eye test with glasses on. Take glasses off, you don't pass the test. Same thing. Augmented genius is a possibility. It's a trend forecast. Robots also get all integrated into as well. Again trend forecast.

Scenario 2:

Political/Economic Turmoil – Future Despair

- Political grid-lock increases social polarization, prevents decisionmaking
- Political, economic, environmental migrations increase ethnic conflicts
- Governments did not anticipate impacts of artificial general intelligence: hence, no strategies to address increasing mass unemployment
- Unemployment exploded in the 2030s leads to 2050 in political turmoil
- Financial systems cannot support ageing societies, financial crises
- World order has deteriorated into a combination of nation-states, mega-corporations, local militias, terrorist groups, and organized crime

Scenario 2. What happens here is also a projection but of different assumptions. It assumes that the ideological, introverted, people of different groups get increasingly polarized because of information warfare. It's not just Russia. A lot of corporations can start doing it, different countries can do it, when they saw that Russia got away with it with the United States, and if I'm in country X, a leader in country Y, cost the effects. It's a lot cheaper than tanks, less environmental pollution, good citizens, what this means though, you would end up with a really paranoid world, not biologically paranoid but behaviorally paranoid. What can you trust? So the political grid-lock increases. The problem here, what's the consequence. The consequence is, most of the serious problems in the world need global decisions like the AI and the rest of the things. You do everything right on the AI and Japan doesn't. You get the impacts still. A lot of the issues, we've got to get right. We've got to get right as a whole human family. But we don't because we're not cutting across systems because we're not trusting each other.

Because we don't get trusted, you got a lot of political, economic and environmental migrations that increase ethnic conflict. You can't have migrations in known area without a conflict, most of the time actually, a lot of conflict. So if you have half the world unemployed and half of the world wants migration, that's a lot of conflict. That makes a current migration problem look like a child's play.

Governments did not anticipate the impacts of artificial general intelligence hence no strategy to address this mass unemployment. Because we think narrow intelligence, you can see the truck drivers getting unemployed. Not all of the robots come in tomorrow morning. It takes a while to do it so you can prepare for that. But when you have general intelligence, that's a shift. It's a phase shift. Governments are not ready for that. One year, they got 10% unemployment and the next month or year they got 50% unemployment. It can't go 10 to 50 without social chaos.

Unemployment explodes in 2030 and in 2050, political turmoil. Financial system cannot support the aging society. It's a financial crisis continuing different directions. World order has deteriorated into a combination of nation states, mega-corporations, local militias, terrorist groups, and organized crime. For your friends who are too optimistic have them read this scenario. It will sober them up.

By the way, organized crime gets twice as much money per year as all of the military budgets combined. I want that to sink in. Think of the entire military operation this year. It's about 1.6-1.7 trillion dollars. Organized crime, we and others figures about 3 to 4 trillion a year. That can buy the best software and talent. This is deadly serious. Think of all those NTs I talked about before. Organized crimes got the money to buy them. So you think you got problems today and it's going to get a lot worse.

In Scenario 2 AI makes this Combination Far More Powerful...

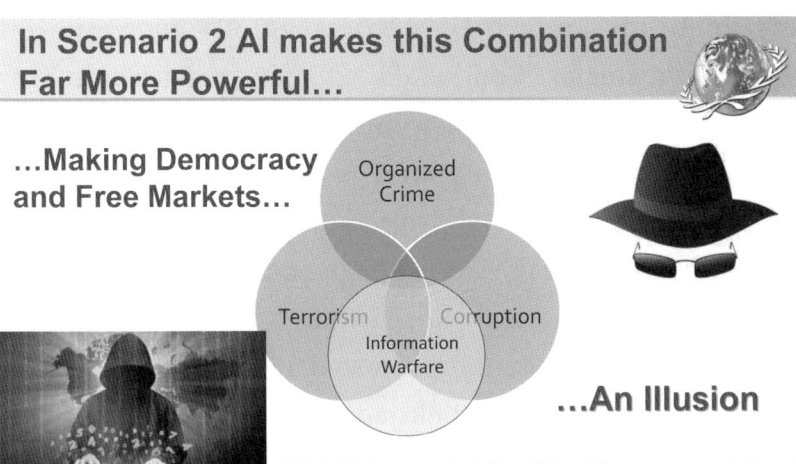

...Making Democracy and Free Markets... ...An Illusion

On top of the organized crime, terrorism and corruption, you would have added a new factor of information warfare. The four of these things together in this scenario makes democracy and free markets an illusion.

Scenario 3:

If Humans Were Free the Self-Actualization Economy

- Governments did anticipate the impacts of artificial general intelligence
- Conducted extensive research on how to phase in universal basic income systems
- Increasing intelligence becomes a goal of education
- Self-employment promoted
- Artists, media moguls, and entertainers helped to foster cultural change from an employment culture to a self-actualization economy.

Now, everything's going to be great. Scenario 3, take a breath, everything is fine. Scenario 3, governments did anticipate the impacts of artificial intelligence and put together strategies. Conducted extensive research on how to phase in universal basic income systems. Increased intelligence becomes a goal of education. Pause. When children don't get enough iron and protein between 3 and 5, the brain doesn't develop enough as it should. You've got periodic starve in North Korea. When East Germany and West Germany got together, it costed a lot of money, a lot of difficulty. You know the whole story. But East Germans were not starved to death periodically for 50 years or whatever. So you've got a much more difficult problem coming up so this idea of augmented intelligence, you've got to learn how to do that because you may need the augmented intelligence of Koreans. You might make a mess if you don't do this.

Self-employment promoted. Artists. This is one of the key variables in this scenario. Artists, media moguls, entertainers helped to foster cultural change for an employment culture to a self-actualization culture. Right now, people say they are who they are because they have a job. I am an economist. I am a futurist. I am a this. Who says, while the boss is here, that's why I am paid for my identity. But if you have to make the shift into the unknown creating your own life, your own world connecting to Internet, that's a big deal for most people. A lot of you are entrepreneurs but for an average person, it's a big deal. So we're going to need the writers in television, movies, so they would help that transition to happen. Otherwise, if a transition happens without this, then they'll have cyber heroin because they have lost their identity, they lost self-respect, and that's a very costly deal.

You all know about the Maslow's hierarchy. Civilization may be going through the same things. This is for the individual. Your safety needs, your physical needs, love and belongings. But the world is, take the world in 1981, more than half the world was in extreme poverty. Today, it's under 10%. And that's where the other 2 billion people are undergoing. So we are winning mostly, but where we're losing is serious. The idea of civilization going in this direction seems to be a plausible idea, so one could actually make a living out of being themselves. Like, for example, I'm doing that right now. Am I at work? Am I at play? Am I at leisure? Well, it's a little bit of three. As far as I know, you're not my boss.

Scenario 3 Your Personal AI Avatar searches the web while you sleep...

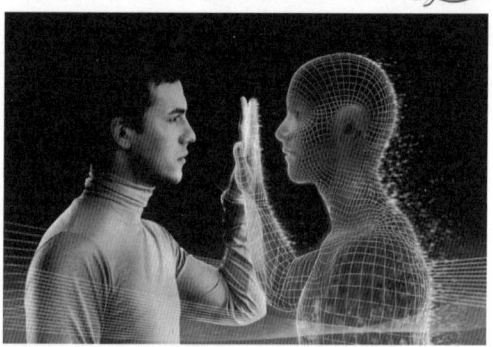

... then wakes you up in the morning ....with all kinds of interesting things to do, some for income, some because the are just fun, and some that are both all with smart contacts if needed.

In this scenario, people have AI avatars. The way AI avatars may come about is BBVA, a bank in Spain, their head of IT has left and he's going to be putting together these avatars. The idea would be while you go to sleep, your AI avatar goes running around the internet, finding all the investment possibilities for you and then the next morning it wakes you up and say "Here's the thing for you to do." Well. Why would banks do this? Because you'll get richer and banks want you to get richer. So they'll give you just like a free e-mail services, you'll start to get these free things. What this means is you can start to make a living as yourself because your AI avatar can come back at morning and say "Here are 15 things that you want to do because it's just cool and here are 15 things to learn for some income. We've already put together these small contracts." All you have to do is just prove that you're in business. You can literally create your future. That's Scenario 3. As I said, this is the most optimistic one.

Steve Jobs and Bill Gates 1991

Consider what these two geniuses created!

Source: reddit.com/r/OldSchoolCool/

By **2030-2050** millions of people could become augmented geniuses, and what could we create?

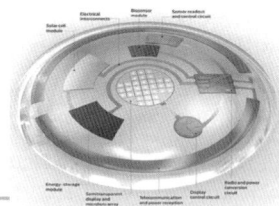

With these augmented geniuses and related issues, consider what these two guys have created. What happens if we have billions, I put millions there just to be very conservative, but if you've got 9 billion people in 2050, or 10 billion people and the workforce of 6 billion and if even a half of them get augmented, because we have a half of the world connected to the internet now, why wouldn't they have augmented as well? That means billions of geniuses. Now, you run a company and everybody is a genius in that company, it's a different management issue. It's a different world.

Some examples of 93 actions assessed

- Make increasing intelligence an objective of education.
- In parallel to STEM education create a hybrid system of self-paced inquiry-based learning for self-actualization, creativity, critical thinking, and human relations using new AI tools.
- Create international standards for narrow and general AI with a governance system to enforce them (maybe similar to the International Atomic Energy Agency – IAEA).
- Produce alternative cash flow projections for universal basic income to see if/when it is financially sustainable.
- Put memes in advertisements to help the cultural transition to new forms of economics and work.
- Create personal AI/Avatars able to match peoples' skills and interests with income opportunities worldwide which can make smart contracts to support self-employment.
- Shift education/learning systems more toward mastering skills than mastering a profession.
- Public/private research should explore the cultural transition for a new social contract between the government and the citizens who potentially could be both unemployed and augmented geniuses.
- Art/media/entertainment leaders should engage the public in anticipating cultural changes due to potential impacts of future technologies.

We've done bunch of workshops, collected suggestions on what should be done. You can read that on the reports. I put out of the 93. These are distilled from all kinds of research, maybe more than 93, just a lot of overlap, you've got to bring them together. Out of the 93, these are my subjective pulling-outs, not scientific. Some examples are here. One, make intelligence or increase intelligence an objective of education. We know a lot about brain functioning. We didn't know when you were a child. Remember we used to think that the brain was a static thing, no more neurons, that's it. We now know that's not true. If you have an average IQ, why can't we get you up to 5-10% more? Why not? We have physical education, right? We all know that. We have mental education too.

In parallel to STEM education, create hybrid systems of self-paced, inquiry-based learning for self-actualization, creativity, critical thinking, and human relations using AI.

I use Korea and Finland in one of these reports as example. Your test scores and Finland's test scores are about the same. But the systems are really different. I mean you guys have made a neurotic generation. You've got to learn everything, right? I'm not telling you that you don't know. Finland as a reverse. All kinds of creativities, and they were worried in Finland, "Okay, we'll do this but we're going to sacrifice test scores." It turned out the test scores were still okay. The more flexible the thinking process is, the easier we do a normal evolution.

Create international standards for narrow intelligence and general artificial intelligence with governance system to enhance them or to enforce them. This is extremely important. Imagine the world today if we didn't have the International Atomic Energy Agency (IAEA). We probably had a few dirty bombs by now. We might not even be here. So it's important to do this, and the impacts of mis-evolution of general intelligence and super intelligence are certainly a big deal as nuclear bombs.

Produce alternative cash flow projections for universal basic income. Why do I stress this? Because I was not too crazy about universal basic income when I started this project, this research. But it became clear that it's a very likely possibility that have shockwaves of unemployment. The social contract today is, you go to school, you do well, you get a job, you behave, you retire. You get a retirement pension and some medical insurance. That's the social contract. Most of the whole world like that. But if you're thrown out to street at 45 and it's not your fault. What does society owe you? You did what you're supposed to do. Here's why we looked at universal basic income as an alternative strategy in Scenario 3 to see how that works because what kind of a society do we want to have? Do we really want to have half of the world thrown out to streets? That's not a cool idea. So there's a lot of ways to do this wrong. So we should begin to study and learn from each other how to do this.

Put memes – memes are ideas that could spread around – in advertisements to help the cultural transition to new forms of economics and work. Create personal AI/Avatars to match peoples' needs and skills. Shift education systems from mastering a profession to mastering skills. Skills will still be important. But particularly professions can change. How many lawyers we got here? I got a couple here. A lot of legal profession is research and paper work, and a lot of them can be done.

That reminds me that I was asked about applying artificial intelligence to a business in generalization so let me pause and give you this. You take your production process, whatever production process it is – whether it's garments, newspapers – doesn't matter. What is your production process? List it out and in each of those. What are the repetitive behaviors? Those repetitive behaviors on each of those things can be AI and that's your marching orders to outside contract I don't do that but somebody else can do that. Few asked me "How do I start changing my organization with AI." Lay out your whole process first. Don't ask an AI company to come in and do it for you. That's no-no. Your job, you got like you'll know what that is. And then what's the repetitive behavior in each step and then each one of those you do the AI, then you will have a process.

Public/private research should explore the cultural transition for a social contract between the government and the citizens who potentially could be both unemployed and augmented geniuses. So imagine in Scenario 2, if you've got a whole lot of people unemployed but they can steal from organized crime, augmented geniuses, you've got much more difficult opponent than you had before. I'm not going to read these things up. The powerpoint will be available to you, so you can go through all these later on. These are different suggestions in different sectors of society. The point here is it's not just STEM education. We've got to do a whole lot of things to make this transition work.

ANI – AGI Global Governance

It is argued that creating rules for governance of AI too soon will stifle its development.

Some AGI experts believe it is possible to have AGI as soon as ten years.

Since it is likely to take ten or more years to
- develop ANI to AGI international agreements
- design and international governance system
- begin implementation

Then it is wise to begin exploring governance approaches **now.**

Here's the AI in governance. It is argued that if we start governance system and standard systems too early, we will stifle the development of AI. Here is the counter. We won't have this done to 10 to 15 years. Imagine getting agreements between China and the United States on artificial intelligence. It's not going to happen in a day. It's going to take 10 to 15 years at least to do this so we're not stopping any innovation in a process. We're learning. Some artificial general intelligence experts believe this possible as soon as 10 years. It might not be but military research tends to be ahead of civilian research so maybe this might be around the corner and happen faster than we think. Since it is likely to take 10 or more years, we've got to develop these international standards now.

Some initial explorations

University of Oxford's Center for the Governance of AI (cultural issues)
United Arab Emirates Ministry of State for AI
UN Interregional Crime and Justice Research Institute's AI Center
Future of Life Institute (identified 26 nation & 6 international strategies)
Partnership on AI
China AI Industry Alliance
AI for Good Foundation
SingularityNet and Decentralized AI Alliance
Harvard Future Society
United Nations University (common platform for papers on AI governance)

Some Potential Governance Models

1. IAEA-like model or WTO-like with enforcement powers
2. IPCC-like model in concert with international treaties
3. International S&T Organization (ISTO) as an online real-time global collective intelligence system; governance by information power GGCC (Global Governance Coordinating Committees) flexible but enforced by national sanctions, ad hoc legal rulings in different countries, and insurance premiums
4. ISO standards affecting international purchases
5. Put different parts of AGI governance under different bodies like ITU, WTO, WIPO
6. TransInstitution

Right now the Millennium Project is discussing if we want to do this study or not, just like the other one we did. These are the players of the systems today that are working on it. Some potential models, you can do the IAEA or the World Trade Organization (WTO) model. Here's a bunch of other models that can be done, so we want to assess the studies, do some scenarios and make the results available.

A few words about the Millennium Project. I used to put together UN organizations, governments, NGOs and foundations, corporations, and universities into a transinstitution. To people who do the work, where the money comes from and the direction comes from all these institution categories, not a majority anyway, which has the advantage that we have to make sense the bottom line because the business is there. We have to make sense politically because the government is there. We have to make values because NGOs are there. We have to make sense internationally because UN is there. But it also means we can act through those organizations. We were studied by the UN years ago and they can't figure out how we do, what we do because we're not acting like a regular organization. Take the best of the each and go forth.

65 Nodes...and two regional networks in Europe and Latin America

are groups of experts and institutions that connect global and local views in:

Nodes identify participants, translate questionnaires and reports, and conduct interviews, special research, workshops, symposiums, and advanced training.

STATE OF THE FUTURE 19.1

Jerome C. Glenn, Elizabeth Florescu, and The Millennium Project Team

Preface
Executive Summary
Ch 1 Global Challenges
Ch 2 2017 State of the Future Index
Ch 3 Future Terrorism & Deterrence
Ch 4 Work/Tech 2050 Scenarios
 and Workshop Strategies
Ch 5 Conclusions
Appendix

We got 65 of nodes around the world. We produce "State of the Future" reports. Again, don't buy the print and download it. We also do methods by the way. We have the largest method production. There's 37 of methods and there is no right way to do future. There are a lot of different methods, and you mix and match your methods as you need. We've done 55 studies so far. This is just to impress you with what we've actually trying to accumulate those research. Of each research we do, leads into the next. Like your brain, new information to your brain, you see how to see with other stuff, hopefully you get smarter as you go along. Same idea. This is the report you can also download. This is printed in Pakistan so you can get the printed book right now but you can also download the electronic version. We put all these together all into a collective intelligence system and you're going to do your own collective intelligence system because consider the brains and the experiences in this room. Imagine if you can actually provide some coherence with the career. It will be great. That's all I got to say. We can have some questions. Thank you.

Artificial Intelligence (AI) and its Impact on the Future of Economy and Society

Questions and Answers

Q Thank you Mr. Glenn for an eye-opening and pretty scary scenario that you got. You started out with a question throughout the history. NTs bringing more jobs. Now we've reached the stage where that can continue. In fact, one of the problems I fear in this scenario is that ultimately in the past, we have transferred the test from lower part of the body to the brain. Now what I want to ask is, can the brain keep up with this thing? 60 years ago, when they started computer programming, few people knew what computer was. Now I fear challenges by my smart phones and you brought up with very good question of increasing intelligence. But 5-10% increase in IQ in the face of this challenge is almost like a Band-Aid and aspirin for a cancer patient. I already see the example of this. You look out throughout the world, the global leaders are not up to the task of what they can do. So that's a very, very low technology area. And if you look at this kind of things, quantum development and technology, can human beings exist as a meaningful existence? In fact, aren't we on the self-destructive mode? Thank you.

A Okay, let's talk about that Band-Aid. Let's say, your eyesight is 20/30. You're going to adjust glasses so you're 20/20. Let's say your eyesight is 20/50. You're going to adjust glasses to it. My point is no matter what your intelligence is, we can augment it. I said 5 to 10%, that was one of the area. There's about 10 areas to increase intelligence, not just one. So each of these added together can be more, so the idea of an augmented genius is plausible.

Now, we all know, the first stuff is used by wealthy people. But then the price comes down and market expands and price comes down and market expands and so forth. So that Band-Aid can be augmented itself. Remember there are 3 scenarios here. There's not one. 3 scenarios. And I would challenge you to read those 3 scenarios at leisure and then ask yourself to question again because a lot of the answers are in there.

If you believe that these problems cannot be addressed, what's the logical conclusion? Do nothing and have cyber heroin or some other version. That's a bad conclusion. Remember Hamlet got poisoned into his ear, so we keep telling next generation, forget it, it's over. They're not going to try. I studied relevant studies for 45 years. There is not a single question or problem there are no answers to. Not a single one. I'm talking about some really nasty stuff. The problem is, which goes to your other part of the question, leaders. We don't have good leadership. We don't have good decision making. That's true. That doesn't mean new forms of leadership can come out. Like the landmine treaty, that's a new form of leadership. A person acting on their own, creating something that actually made a difference. It's important what we believe. The only contribution the United States is making in philosophy, it's called pragmatic philosophy which basically says we don't know the truth but we can know if it works. So if it works, we call it true. If it doesn't work, we say it's false. It doesn't work to be pessimistic. It does work to look at negative stuff but it doesn't work to be pessimistic. We've been studying indicators for the future civilization again in the Millennium Project for over 20 years. Yes, 20 years. I can tell you, on that data, we're winning more than losing. So we have no right to be pessimistic. But where we're losing is deadly serious as you point out. So we have no right to go to sleep either. To me, that's the rational position. We want a hard-headed, pragmatic, serious idealist. We don't need pessimism. Thank you.

Q Thank you very much for an impressive, eye-opening and confusing future. I'm just trying to put things in the perspective. You have been working in that business for so many years. You just mentioned 45 and the Millennium Project is like 26 years or something. As you go along trying to put things into your perspective, how accurate were you? I mean you had enough time to judge some of your earlier results and I assume also you're improving as you're learning more about the methodology and approaches, so how confident are you about your predictions?

A We wanted to be wrong about all predictions on thermonuclear war. Sometimes you do a scenario or story or projection to be proven wrong. Like climate change. We don't want to get to a thousand apart for million. That's scary. We're gone. Sometimes you alert. The idea isn't to be accurate but is to be useful. Is it useful to give a warning? Yes. Have my warnings been taken seriously? A lot of them have. If you want to know the conventional sense that I talked about, there's a book called "Future Mind" that I wrote 30 years ago. And in there I talked about the TOK, the tree of knowledge. The TOK is what we have in our pocket today and I described 30 years ahead of the time, the TOK, the smart phone. Also, information warfare you read on the defense chapter, you take out the word the U.S. are putting to Russia and it reads like the present tense unfortunately. So unfortunately I've been writing some negative areas that I would like to have been wrong in. But again I jokingly say we'll take bets. We'll do that but it's none of our business to predict to say X will happen. It's to say X will happen if you don't do something. Y could happen if you do something. So, "Are you useful or not?" will be more precise question to ask than "Are you right about it or not?" And one evaluation of useful is do you get invited back to give another talk in Korea.

Q May I throw out one question to you for the interest of our audience? As a renowned futurist, what would you say about the future of Korea? Do you think Korea will be better place in 2050 than today? I think this is a pretty tough question.

A That's alright. This goes back to my friend's, from Egypt, question. The object is will you take seriously, Korea, the warnings laid out and act in response to those. How you act is your own judgement but at least these are warnings. If you're dealing with unification down the road, are you going to look at how to augment intelligence. I don't want to say what percent but a lot of North Koreans are mentally retarded. It has nothing to do with genetics. It's got to do with being starved. They had the genes to be intelligent. They're your brothers and sisters but they haven't been treated nicely so their brains haven't developed. If you just reunite and you don't plan ahead on this, thenI would predict if you don't do it, you'll get a financial problem bigger than Germany had. I think that Korea has a number of interesting situations. One, by having Japan, China, North Korea around, it's sort of keep showing under your toes. It's hard for you to fall asleep. It's not like Hawaii. You know you're on the Pacific. It has very nice weather. You can relax. You have hard time relaxing here, which means that your brain is more active than average in my judgement.

Two, because you've had such rapid change, you understand rapid change is possible. I would say that as a culture. Korea is more future-looking. When I first came here, I stayed at Shilla Hotel. As you know there's a bus that goes to Shilla and 5 major hotels to load people. And I was there with SBS on media and saw a big banner "The Future of Tele-Communications" or something. The next place the bus went to "The Future Something-else." I'm not kidding you. I can pass a lie detector test. All 5 five-star hotels had "The Future of Something." I said "What's going on here?"

Now, there's a part of your story that is, maybe not totally known, remember Park Chung-hee, elementary school teacher, created the greatest economic miracle so far. That's pretty unusual. There was a cold war going on and there was another futurist named Herman Kahn, who invented scenarios. He was one of the top futurists in my time and he hung out with Park Chung-hee a lot of times. You can check this out. Now, the trouble is that people who didn't like him did not want to hear the story. This is being recorded isn't it? Well, it was nice knowing you all. But this is an important story, you should know. The people who don't like Park Chung-hee – because you know, he was a pretty tough character, right? – don't want to be reminded necessarily of how much success he had. The people who like him don't want to be reminded that an American had something to do with it. An American futurist. That's why I bring it up. I would say that when people say what is the value of futurists' research, this story is one of the best stories. But you haven't heard about it because no one is interested in having that story. It has been written up as a book.

You have a tradition here of listening to crazy people like me. Right? I mean you invited me. I didn't ask. I didn't even know what you were doing. But you have an openness that will serve you well if you don't get too pessimistic. But you don't want to have optimism without tested by pessimism. Pessimism is important. But it's not the food. It's sort of the spice.

I think Korea can do very well because you've already proven to yourself what's possible. I mean look at Korea. The classic example is Ghana versus South Korea. It's used by people around the world. But what you've got to do is to make a transition because before you're in a catch-up economy. That's what they did, we can do that. You've done it. You caught up. Not in everything but you caught up enough that you're not in a catch-up economy. You're there now. You're on equal playing field with the major powers of the world. You know how big is China but in the sense of knowing, having knowledge on artificial intelligence and all these other things, we're together now. You have the advantage of being on your toes because of your geographic position and because of your history. You know what's possible. I want you to have a great future. Don't let pessimism throw you in jail. Thank you.

미·중, 한·일 무역분쟁과 세계 무역체제의 미래

U.S.-China, Korea-Japan Trade Disputes and the Global Trading System

제프리 샷
(Jeffrey J. Schott)

제프리 샷

Jeffrey J. Schott

미국 피터슨국제경제연구소(PIIE)의 국제무역정책과 경제제재 분야 수석연구위원(Senior Fellow). 미국 재무부에서 국제무역 및 에너지 정책 분야 전문가로 오랫동안 근무하였으며 프린스턴대학교(Princeton University)와 조지타운대학교(Georgetown University)에서 객원교수를 역임. 현재 미국 국무부의 국제경제정책 자문위원으로 활동하고 있음.

미·중, 한·일 무역분쟁과 세계 무역체제의 미래

제프리 샷
피터슨 국제 경제 연구소 (PIIE) Senior Fellow

전광우 이사장님과 사공일 명예이사장님께 감사드립니다. 저는 여러 동료와 함께 세계경제연구원과 오랫동안 유익하고 좋은 관계를 유지해 왔습니다. 훌륭한 분들을 모신 뜻깊은 자리에 저를 변함없이 초대해 주시고 발표할 수 있는 기회를 주셔서 영광으로 생각합니다.

오늘의 강연 제목은 '미·중, 한·일 무역분쟁과 세계 무역체제의 미래'입니다. 제목도 길고 주제도 복잡합니다. 위의 제목에서 일부만 떼어서 강연을 해도 1시간은 얘기할 수 있을 정도입니다. 반면 저에게 주어진 시간은 30분인데요, 이 시간 동안 제목에 담긴 3개의 주제를 하나로 연결하고 여러분의 고견을 들으려고 합니다. 이를 통해 오늘 제가 미처 다루지 못한 주제에 대해 문제제기를 할 수 있기를 바랍니다.

우선 미·중 무역분쟁부터 시작하겠습니다. 오래전부터 계속된 분쟁인데, 논의의 편의를 위해 트럼프 대통령이 대통령에 취임한 2019년 1월 19일부터 양국의 무역분쟁을 살펴보도록 하겠습니다.

미국이 중국과의 무역전쟁을 시작한 이유는 무역역조를 시정하기 위함이었습니다. 경제학자들은 양국의 무역 불균형이 심각한 문제는 아니라고 봅니다. 그럼에도 세간에서는 미국의 막대한 상품 무역적자에 대한 우려가 컸습니다. 트럼프 행정부는 중국에서 미국산 제품의 구매를 늘리는 동시에, 그동안 교역과 투자를 왜곡했던 중국의 보조금 및 규제정책을 바로잡고자 했습니다. 특히 기존 산업에서 이 같은 왜곡이 두드러졌습니다. 초기에는 철강 산업에 초점을 맞추었습니다. 이후에는 첨단산업으로 새 무역정책의 폭을 넓혔습니다.

초기에는 미국과 중국 모두 무역분쟁이 오래가지 않을 것으로 보았습니다. 중국이 미국기업에 대한 차별적 규제를 철폐하겠다고 소폭 양보하면 분쟁이 끝나리라는 예상이었습니다. 그러나 흥미롭게도 실제 결과는 달랐습니다. 지난 5~6분기 동안 격렬한 분쟁이 계속되었는데, 이 기간 동안 트럼프 대통령의 트위터를 보면 조울병(manic and depression)이 연상될 정도입니다. 트위터 하나에 미국의 입장이 손바닥처럼 뒤집히기도 했습니다. 가령 올해 4월만 하더라도 양국이 합의에 이를 것처럼 보였습니다. 그러다가 협상이 급작스레 결렬되더니, 얼마 지나지 않아 대화가 재개되었습니다. 이 같은 호재에 시장이 긍정적으로 반응하면 또다시 협상이 깨졌습니다. 조울병의 주기가 다시 시작되는 것입니다. 이 같은 양상이 지금까지 계속되었습니다. 현재는 조증과 우울증 중에서 전자의 단계입니다. 양국 정부의 회동을 통해 협상을 다시 본궤도에 올려놓으려는 것입니다. 특히 10월 10일이나 11일의 워싱턴에서 열리는 양국 고위급 회담에서 최소한 잠정 합의라도 도출해서, 서로간 관세의 보복적 인상을 막으려는 모습입니다.

이 같은 갈등에는 비용이 뒤따릅니다. 미·중 무역분쟁의 장기화 결과 상호 불신이 악화되어 향후 양국 간의 경제협력이 어려워졌습니다. 또한 한국을 비롯한 여러 국가와 지역에도 파급효과를 불러왔으며, WTO 체제에도 부정적인 영향을 미쳤습니다.

그럼 간략하게나마 미·중 무역분쟁의 현주소를 살펴보겠습니다. 양국이 이행하겠다고 위협한 무역조치가 12월 15일이 실제로 적용된다면, 미국으로 수입되는 중국산 제품의 97%에 대해 평균 24%의 관세가 부과됩니다. 무역분쟁이 개시되기 전 미국이 최혜국대우(MFN) 원칙에 따라 중국산 제품에 적용한 3%보다 훨씬 더 높은 세율입니다.

트럼프는 2016년 대선 때 중국산 제품에 35~45%의 관세를 부과하여 미국 시장에서의 가격을 높이겠다고 지지자들에게 공약했습니다. 그리고 자신의 공약을 지켰습니다. 미국이 위협한 관세 인상이 10월 15일과 12월 15일에 단행되면 중국간 제품에 대한 관세가 25%로 증가하게 됩니다. 사실상 모든 중국산 제품이 15%에서 30%에 이르는 보복적 초고관세의 적용을 받는 것입니다.

이 같은 미국의 움직임에 중국도 맞불을 놓았지민, 보나 신숭한 모습입니다. 미국산 제품에 대한 관세를 인상하면 중국 기업의 비용부담이 늘어날 수 있습니다. 미국산 제품의 가격이 인상되면 중국 소비자도 피해를 입고, 미국에서 수입된 부품을 쓰는 중국 세쿰의 가격도 올라갑니다. 중국은 12월 15일에 미국산 제품의 69%를 대상으로 보복적 관세를 부과하겠다고 밝혔습니다.

그러나 대체 수입원이 없는 항공기나 약품 등은 보복 대상에서 제외했습니다. 이들 분야에서는 중국 제품의 경쟁력을 유지하기 위해 미국산 제품이 필요하기 때문입니다.

무역분쟁 전까지 중국은 미국산 제품에 대해 MFN 원칙에 따라 8%의 관세를 적용했습니다. 그러나 앞으로는 25~26%의 무역가중평균 관세가 부과됩니다. 미국과 같은 방향의 조치입니다. 그 결과 중국 시장에서 미국산 제품이 타국의 수입품에 비해 가격 및 접근성에서 불리한 위치에 놓이게 됩니다. 게다가 중국이 타국의 수입품에 대한 MFN 관세를 낮추면서 미국산 제품의 경쟁력은 더욱 악화되었습니다. 중국정부가 타국의 수입품에 대한 관세는 인하하고, 미국 제품에 대한 관세는 인상하면서 26% 관세 이상의 피해를 미국이 입게 되었습니다.

이 같은 25%의 관세 차별로 인해 대두를 비롯한 농산품에서 미국 제품의 수요는 줄고 타국 제품의 수요는 늘었습니다. 큰 폭의 수입선 대체는 다른 분야에서도 나타나고 있습니다. 물론 미국의 관세 인상으로 인해 중국산 제품도 미국 시장에서 이 같은 수입선 대체의 피해를 입었습니다. 그러나 미국산 제품의 수요 증가로 이어지지는 않았습니다. 오히려 관세 전쟁과 중국의 대미(對美) 수출 감소로 인해 동아시아와 동남아시아 국가들의 대미 수출이 늘어났습니다.

즉 중국은 미국산 제품에 대한 관세는 인상하고 타국에 대한 관세를 낮추는 모습을 보였습니다. 그 결과 미국과 중국에서 보호무역주의가 점증했습니다. 양국간 수출입액은 감소했습니다.

미국의 대중 무역적자가 감소하기는 했지만, 막대한 상품 무역적자 규모를 감안하면 극히 미미한 수준입니다. 미국의 중국산 제품 수입이 줄기는 했지만, 대신 동남아시아 국가 제품의 수입이 늘었습니다. 또한 미국의 글로벌 무역적자 규모에는 큰 변화가 없었고 오히려 소폭 증가했습니다. 이는 관세전쟁 때문이라기보다, 미국의 경제가 비교적 탄탄한데다 달러화 가치가 올랐기 때문입니다. 그 결과 미국은 엄청난 수준의 상품 무역적자를 기록하게 되었습니다.

결국 미국으로서는 이 같은 손해를 입으면서 굳이 무역분쟁을 개시할 이유가 없었던 셈입니다. 다만 하나의 예외가 있습니다. 트럼프는 대선후보 시절 관세를 인상하겠다고 공약했고 실제로 이를 이행했습니다. 트럼프는 이 같이 지지자에 대한 약속을 지키는 것이 2020년의 대선 승리를 위해 필요하다고 보고 있습니다. 그 점에서 무역분쟁은 경제적 요소 뿐 아니라 정치적 요소도 포함합니다. 2020년 11월의 대선이 다가올수록 정치적 계산이 경제적 이익보다 중요해질 것입니다.

현재 양국은 협상을 통한 잠정협정 도출로 관세의 보복적 인상을 막고 현재의 분쟁을 최소한 휴전상태로 전환하려고 합니다. 이를 위해 중국은 미국산 제품의 수입을 늘리고 외국인 투자와 지적재산권에서 미국의 요구를 들어줄 수도 있습니다. 중국은 자국의 기존 법령 및 내년 1월에 발효될 예정인 법을 통해 상기의 양보에 조치를 이행할 수도 있습니다. 심지어 외국인 투자나 지적재산권 보호에서 이전보다 전향적인 입장을 보일 수도 있습니다.

그러나 중국이 위와 같이 양보해서 양국이 합의에 이르더라도 오래 가지 못할 것입니다. 민주당과 공화당 모두 미국이 중국에 굴복해서는 안된다는 입장이기 때문입니다. 만일 미국이 중국과 합의하면, 양당에서는 미국이 중국에게 너무 유화적으로 나왔다고 비판할 가능성이 높습니다. 대선을 앞두고 유권자 표를 의식한 행보입니다. 저는 양국이 수주나 수개월 내에 합의에 도달하여 지금까지의 관세 인상을 부분적으로나마 철회하고, 두 나라가 2개월 내에 이행하겠다고 공언한 관세 인상을 중지하기를 바랍니다.

그러나 이 같은 합의가 얼마나 오래 갈지 의문스럽습니다. 미국이 내년 대선을 앞두고 정치적 불확실성이 커지면 합의가 결렬되고 무역분쟁이 원점으로 다시 돌아갈 수도 있습니다.

현재까지 관세인상으로 인한 순효과를 보면, 미국과 중국 모두 GDP가 소폭 감소했습니다. 미국과 중국은 경제 대국입니다. 미국이 5,000억 달러의 중국산 제품에 25%의 관세를 부과하더라도 그 증가액은 1,250억 달러에 불과합니다. 20조 달러에 달하는 중국의 경제규모를 감안하면 거시적으로 볼 때 비교적 미미한 수준입니다.

이 같은 수치를 들어 일각에서는 "관세인상을 우려할 필요가 없다"가 주장합니다. 그러나 이는 단순히 관세문제만이 아닙니다. 이 자리에 기업인도 많이 와 계시는데요, 관세전쟁이 진정으로 우려되는 이유는 정책의 예측 가능성을 떨어뜨려 기업의 투자 불확실성을 크게 증가시키기 때문입니다. 기업들은 신규 투자를 보류하고 현 사태를 관망하고 있습니다. 그 결과 경제성장에 필요한 투자가 이루어지지 않고 있습니다. 관세인상이 가져오는 공급사슬 충격에 대비해 기업들은 추가로 공급업체나 재고를 확보하고 있는데, 이는 투자의 효율성을 떨어뜨립니다. 한 공급업체의 경우 정부의 제재정책 때문에 공급선이 막혔습니다.

이는 경제적 효율성의 하락으로 이어집니다. 경제의 생산성이 떨어지고 중기 차원의 경제 성장률도 감소합니다. 관세 인상의 단계적 효과를 훨씬 뛰어넘는 부정적 효과가 투자에서 나타나고 있습니다. 미국과 중국 뿐 아니라 다른 국가들도 피해자입니다. 이들 국가는 미국 및 중국과 교역하고 있는 데다, 관세 인상으로 인한 세계경제의 불확실성에 똑같이 노출되어 있기 때문입니다.

미국은 제대로 된 사전준비 없이 현재의 무역전략을 이행했습니다. 그 결과 미국과 중국 모두 손해를 입었습니다. 미국의 경우 단기적 영향도 중요합니다. 내년에 대선이 있기 때문입니다. 대선을 앞두고 미국의 성장률이 떨어지면, 누가 대통령에 당선될지에 영향을 줄 수 있습니다.

대선에서는 통상 현직 대통령이 유리합니다. 경제가 좋을 때는 더욱 그렇습니다. 트럼프 대통령은 대선을 앞두고 미국 경제가 일정수준 이상 성장할 수 있도록 전력을 다할 것입니다. 고용상황은 매우 양호합니다. 금리도 낮기 때문에, 현 경제상황을 유지만 한다면 트럼프 대통령은 높은 확률로 재선에 성공할 것입니다. 트럼프의 탄핵과 관련한 지난 2일 간의 상황에 대해서는 일단 여기까지만 얘기하겠습니다. 대신 추후에 기회가 되면 언급하도록 하겠습니다. 오늘의 강연은 경제가 주제인데, 언젠가는 미국경제의 성장세가 둔화될 수밖에 없습니다. 트럼프가 금리를 인하하라고 연준을 강력하게 압박하는 이유입니다. 그러나 트럼프의 요구대로 연준이 여러 차례에 걸쳐 큰 폭으로 금리를 인하할 가능성은 거의 없습니다.

미·중 무역분쟁에서 장기화될 가능성은 높고 해결 가능성은 낮은 문제가 하나 있습니다. 바로 첨단제품의 교역과 투자를 둘러싼 마찰입니다. 이는 화웨이나 ZTE를 넘어선 문제입니다. 미국은 중국이 해킹을 통해 미국의 기업을 도용했다고 보고 있습니다. 이에 맞서 미국은 2018년에 일련의 관련법을 입법화했습니다. 외국인의 미국 내 직접투자에 대해 첨단산업을 중심으로 심사를 대폭 강화하는 것이 골자입니다.

이같이 강화된 심사 때문에 중국의 대미 직접투자가 사실상 끊겼습니다. 다른 국가의 대미 투자는 그 정도로까지 급락하지는 않았지만, 이전보다 투자에 신중해진 것은 사실입니다. 꼭 중국 기업 투자에 대한 미국의 심사를 염려해서가 아닙니다. 그보다는 미국 경제의 성장세가 약화되고, 자동차를 비롯한 여러 업종의 상황 및 소비자 선호가 바뀌고 있기 때문입니다. 상기 변화로 인해 미국의 해외투자도 영향을 받고 있습니다. 미국 의회는 외국 기업의 미국 내 투자에 대한 심사를 강화하는 법과 더불어 수출통제개혁법을 통과시켰습니다. 전략적으로 중요한 첨단 제품과 기술이 해외로 빠져나가 중국 손에 들어가는 것을 막기 위한 법입니다. 이 법에 따라 미·중 간의 직접적인 제품교역뿐 아니라 한·미, 미·일 간 교역도 보다 엄격한 심사의 대상이 됩니다. 한국이나 일본이 미국으로부터 수입한 기술 및 제품이 중국으로 유출될 수도 있다는 우려 때문입니다. 미국 정부는 작년에 입법화된 수출통제개혁법에 따라 관련 규정을 마련하고 있는데, 이 규정에서 신기술(emerging technology)과 핵심 기술(foundational technology)를 어떻게 정의하는가에 따라 미국 및 해외 기업 간 교역이 아주 엄격한 심사의 대상이 될 수 있습니다.

혹시 이 같은 기술의 정의가 어떻게 되는지 감이 오지 않는다면 여러분만 그런 것이 아닙니다. 저 뿐만 아니라 미국 정부도 마찬가지입니다. 그러나 현재의 심사나 수출통제보다는 훨씬 까다로워질 것입니다. 미국정부가 첨단 제품 및 기술의 유출을 얼만큼 철저히 감시하는가에 따라 주요 기술이 얼만큼 포괄적으로 정의될지 결정될 것입니다.

이는 상당히 복잡한 문제로서, 미국과 중국에서 정치적으로 아주 뜨거운 쟁점입니다. 그리고 단순히 경제 문제가 아닌 국가 안보 문제입니다. 수출개혁통제법의 통과 과정에서 미국 의회에서는 반중 정서가 고조된 반면, 중국은 크게 반발하는 모습입니다.

첨단 기술을 둘러싼 갈등은 무역 협상으로 해결할 수 있는 사안이 아닙니다. 설령 무역분쟁이 일단락된다고 해도 이 문제는 아시아 태평양 국가 간의 관계에서 중요한 변수로 남아있을 것입니다.

미·중 갈등을 고조시킬 수 있는 세 번째 요인은 미국이 이란, 북한, 베네수엘라 등의 국가에 가하고 있는 경제 제재입니다. 특히 이란과 베네수엘라에 대한 석유 제재가 문제입니다. 미국은 두 나라가 석유 수출로 거두는 수입원을 철저하게 차단하는 정책을 시행하고 있습니다. 그리고 이란과 베네수엘라 원유의 상당수를 중국이 수입하고 있습니다. 지금까지 미국은 이란으로부터 석유를 수입하고 있는 국가를 대상으로 원유수입 금지조치에 대한 예외를 인정했습니다. 그러나 금년 5월부터 현물교환이나 채무구제 등 교역의 형식을 막론하고, 이란으로부터 원유를 수입하거나 운송하는 에너지 기업, 해운회사, 금융기관은 매우 강력한 미국의 경제재제 대상이 됩니다. 사실상 미국 달러화를 사용하는 시장에서 거래가 금지되는 셈인데, 글로벌 경제로부터 차단되는 것과 마찬가지입니다.

미국 정보기관에서는 중국 석유화공(Sinopec)이나 중국석유가스공사(SNPC) 등의 중국 주요 국유기업이 이란과의 거래에 연루되어 있다는 증거를 입수했습니다. 만일 이런 중국 기업에 대한 제재가 부과된다면 미·중 무역분쟁은 한 단계 더 높은 수준으로 격화될 것입니다. 이는 미국에도 이득이 되지 않기 때문에, 미정부에서도 조심스러운 모습을 보였습니다. 미국의 이란이나 북한 정책에 중국이 어느 정도 협력을 하고 있는데, 이는 미국의 정책을 따라가는 편이 자국에도 이득이라고 중국이 계산한 결과입니다. 덕분에 양국 간 긴장은 완화되었습니다. 중국은 미국 경제제재를 협상의 지렛대로 삼아 이란으로부터 낮은 가격에 원유를 구입했습니다. 이란은 대중 원유수출을 유지하기 위해 큰 폭으로 원유값을 할인해야 했습니다.

반면 미국이 작정하고 중국과 대립하려고 마음먹고 이를 실천에 옮길 가능성도 있습니다. 제가 관련 글도 쓴 적이 있는데, 그 직후에 재무부에서 미국의 제재대상이 되는 중국 국적 선박의 추가 명단을 발표했습니다. 이란과의 원유거래에 연루되었다는 것이 이유였습니다. 금주의 며칠 전에 있던 발표였습니다. 원하시면 더 자세히 설명드릴 수도 있는데요, 불난 집에 부채질하는 상황을 피해야 한다는 것이 제 요지입니다. 즉 다른 문제의 악화가 미·중 무역분쟁을 격화시켜서는 안 된다는 것입니다.

제 발표시간이 길어지고 있는 것 같은데, 한·일 무역분쟁에 관해 간단히 언급하겠습니다. 한국과 일본 양국도 미·중 무역분쟁과 그로 인한 공급사슬 교란의 피해를 입었기 때문에, 두 무역분쟁은 상호 연관되었다고 볼 수 있습니다.

만일 여러분이 기업인이거나, 한국 경제성장의 미래를 걱정하는 분이라면 현 상황을 더욱 악화시키는 정책은 이행하지 않을 것입니다. 미·중 무역분쟁으로 인한 피해에 대처하는 것만도 벅차기 때문입니다. 한·일 교역이 한국 경제에서 차지하는 비중은 10% 이하지만, 한국에게 중요한 핵심 분야에 집중되어 있습니다. 이 점에서 양국 간의 해묵은 정치·외교·문화적 갈등을 관리할 수 있는 방법을 찾아야 합니다.

일본의 대한(對韓) 직접투자가 한국 경제에 차지하는 비중은 한·일 무역이 한국 경제에서 차지하는 비중보다도 훨씬 더 높습니다. 투자액이 500억 달러에 달하는데, 이는 한국의 유치하는 해외투자의 20%에 해당합니다. 절반은 서비스업에, 절반은 제조업에 대한 투자입니다. 500억 달러라면 한국 경제에 상당한 영향을 미칠 수 있는 액수입니다.

저는 한·일 갈등의 원인을 진단하고자 하는 것이 아닙니다. 이는 여러분께서 더 정확하게 분석할 수 있을 것입니다. 그러나 이 말씀은 드리고 싶습니다. 제 가족도 전쟁의 피해자로서, 전시에 강제 수용소에 갇혀 일부가 사망했습니다. 그 점에서 한국의 입장을 이해합니다. 그러나 양국의 정치 지도자들은 두 나라 간 고질적인 정치적 문제를 극복하고 그 효과를 관리함으로써 부정적 여파를 최소화해야 할 책무를 지고 있습니다. 그러나 현재는 이 같은 모습을 볼 수 없는데, 그 책임은 3개의 국가에 있습니다. 한·일 갈등은 한국과 일본의 국가안보 이익 뿐 아니라 미국의 경제안보 이익에도 부정적 영향을 미쳤습니다. 미·중 무역분쟁으로 이미 교란된 글로벌 공급사슬이 한·일 간 마찰로 인해 한층 더 타격을 입을 수 있습니다. 한국과 일본의 국가안보나 경제적 이익을 감안하면, 두 나라는 상대 국가의 상품과 서비스에 차별적 조치를 시행하는 것을 자제해야 합니다.

그동안 한국과 일본은 상대를 여러 차례 WTO에 제소했습니다. 여기까지는 괜찮습니다. 문제는 기존의 WTO 협정 하에서는 양국이 패소할 가능성이 높습니다. 판결이 나오기까지 몇 달이나 몇 년이 걸리는 반면, 그로 인한 피해는 현재 진행형입니다. 그 점에서 상대국을 WTO에 제소하는 것은 현 상황의 타개나 관리에 도움이 되지 못합니다.

양국은 역내에서 같은 안보 위협에 직면하고 있습니다. 그만큼 양자 협력의 필요성이 시급한데, 이 협력이 오랜 과거사 문제

때문에 차질을 빚는 일이 있어서는 안 됩니다. 물론 문재인 대통령과 아베 총리는 여러 요인을 고려하여 자국의 정책을 결정했을 것입니다. 그러나 미국인 입장에서 보면 양국의 현 정책은 이행되지 말았어야 했습니다. 역효과만 불러오기 때문입니다. 저는 한국이나 일본의 정책을 평가할 입장에 있지 않습니다. 그러나 미국 정책을 평가할 수는 있을 것 같습니다. 한국과 일본의 조치보다 미국의 부작위가 더 큰 문제입니다. 미국에게 핵심적인 안보 동맹에 균열이 갈 때까지 방치한 것이 현재까지 트럼프 행정부의 최대 실책입니다.

저는 워싱턴에서 50년 가까이 활동했습니다. 그동안 역대 미국 행정부는 변함없이 주요 동맹국의 대화를 통해 서로 간 차이를 극복하고자 했습니다. 동맹국과의 마찰이 미국 국가안보를 손상하는 것을 피하기 위함이었습니다. 그러나 현 상황을 보면, 워싱턴에 미 국무부가 소재하고 있음에도 국무부는 지나치게 소극적인 모습입니다. 이는 미국의 안보에 심각한 문제이며 그 중대함을 인식해야 합니다. 그러나 현재는 이 같은 상황 인지가 이루어지고 있지 않습니다.

안보 문제가 경제 문제에 우선합니다. 그러나 한국과 일본이 대치하는 상황에서 미국이 이에 관여하지 않는다면, 미·중 무역분쟁의 파급효과를 관리할 수 있는 능력도 제한적일 수밖에 없습니다. 한국 입장에서도 역내 협력과 교역 및 투자를 촉진하여 미·중 무역분쟁의 충격을 완화할 수 있는 여지가 줄어듭니다. 그러나 현재까지 한·미·일 정부의 행보를 보면, 이 같은 사실을 세 정부가 제대로 인식하지 못하는 것으로 보입니다.

저는 경제 및 안보 차원에서 한국과 미국 간 관계를 발전시키기 위해 지난 20년간 많은 노력을 기울였습니다. 한미 FTA와 양국 간 우호관계의 증진에도 힘써 왔습니다. 미일 동맹도 마찬가지입니다. 양국의 안보 관계를 발전시켜 두 나라 간 조금의 이견도 없도록 해야 합니다. 약간이라도 동맹과의 관계에 금이 가는 일이 있어서는 안 됩니다. 그 점에서 미국 정부의 책임이 막중합니다.

이제 강의의 막바지에 접어들었습니다. 제가 지금까지 말씀드린 여러 사안을 하나로 연결시켜야 하는데, 어떻게 이을 수 있을지 저도 고민중입니다.

현재의 상황이 세계 무역체제에 갖는 함의를 살펴보겠습니다. 현재까지는 주로 부정적 영향을 미쳤습니다. 미·중 무역분쟁에서 두 나라가 이행한 일련의 조치는 WTO 협정에 위반됩니다. 회원국간 갈등을 중재하고 신뢰를 증진하는 WTO의 취지에도 맞지 않습니다. 미·중 무역분쟁이 여러 문제를 낳았습니다. 그럼에도 미국은 이를 역내 및 다자 차원에서 해결하려는 모습을 보이고 있지 않습니다. 동맹국과 협력하려는 노력도 부족했습니다. 오히려 미국은 이들 국가를 공격의 대상으로 삼았습니다. 또한 미·중 협력의 장이 될 수 있는 WTO 등의 다자체제를 부정했습니다.

이 같은 갈등은 WTO 체제와 규칙기반 세계질서를 위협에 빠뜨렸습니다. 분쟁 당사국이 협상 테이블에 복귀하고 세계무역 규칙을 시대의 변화에 맞추어 개정할 수 있는 여지를 차단했기 때문입니다. 몇몇 예외를 제외하면, 세계무역 규칙은 1990년대 초에 제정된 후 현재까지 그대로 이어져 내려왔습니다. 그동안 세계무역은 크게 변화했음에도, WTO는 이 규칙을 개정하는 데 실패했습니다. 그래서 회원국들은 WTO 체제에서 벗어나 역내 차원에서 무역 규칙을 개정하고자 했습니다. 한미 FTA만 해도 WTO 협정을 여러 분야에서 상당부분 업그레이드했습니다. 덕분에 향후 다자나 글로벌 차원에서 WTO 협정의 개정에 대한 논의가 재개될 때 선례로서 참고할 수 있게 되었습니다. TPP(환태평양 무역협정)도 한미 FTA를 상당부분 참고했습니다. 덕분에 미국의 가치와 더불어 교역 및 경제적 관행도 아시아태평양 국가로 전파할 수 있었습니다. 그러나 트럼프의 취임 후 불과 4일만에 미국이 TPP에서 탈퇴했습니다. 지금까지 미국의 무역 정책은 이 결정의 부작용을 수습하는 데 맞춰졌다고 해도 과언이 아닙니다. USMCA(미국-멕시코-캐나다 무역협정)도 자동차 산업을 보호하려는 일부 장치를 제외하면 TPP를 그대로 이식했습니다. 얼마 전 타결된 미일 FTA만 해도 TPP의 농업협정을 고스란히 가져왔습니다. 비록 농업분야에서는 TPP에 비해 미진하기는 하지만, 대신 다른 분야에서는 미국이 TPP 수준의 양보를 일본으로부터 받아냈습니다. 그 점에서 한미 FTA는 여러 잡음에도 불구하고 긴재힌 모습입니다. 곧이 힌미 FTA가 후퇴한 부분을 꼽자면 한국의 대미 철강수출 쿼터가 1/3 감소했다는 것입니다. 그러나 그 영향은 크지 않을 것입니다.

현재 전세계 각 나라에서 보호무역주의가 점증하고 있습니다. 보호무역주의는 WTO 협정에 위반됩니다. WTO 협정 자체가 보호무역주의를 방지하고자 탄생했습니다. 문제는 중국의 WTO 협정 위반이 아닙니다. 오히려 중국은 지금까지 WTO 협정을 대체로 준수해 왔습니다. 준수하지 않았을 때는 미국이 중국을 상대로 WTO에 제소했는데, 거의 대부분 미국이 승소했습니다. 예외라면 반덤핑관세 관련 일부 사건에서 패소한 정도입니다. 라이트하이저 대사(미국 무역대표부 대표)가 이를 불편하게 생각할 수 있겠군요.

중국의 가장 큰 문제는 정부의 정책이 무역과 투자를 왜곡하고 있다는 점입니다. 이 정책들은 WTO 협정의 공백이나 모호한 부분을 파고들고 있습니다. 또한 중국은 기존 WTO 협정을 우회하거나 편법적으로 활용하고 있습니다. WTO의 다자무역협정을 시대의 변화에 맞추어 개정하지 못한 폐해가 여기서 드러납니다. 이 같은 실패의 대가가 미·중 간 무역갈등을 비롯한 여러 분쟁에서 나타나고 있습니다.

WTO 협정을 개정하려면 주요 교역국가 간 협력이 필요합니다. 여기서 오늘 강연의 모든 주제를 아우를 수 있을 것 같습니다. 미국과 중국이 협력하지 않는 한, 그리고 한국과 일본을 비롯한 주요 교역국이 WTO 협정의 개정에 참여하지 않는 한 새로운 WTO 질서를 수립할 수 없습니다. 미·중 갈등이나 한·일 갈등이 격화될수록 역내 및 다자차원에서 무역체제를 발전시키기가 어려워집니다. WTO 협정을 업데이트하려면 주요 분야에서 여러 국가의 정책이나 입장이 바뀌어야 합니다. 시급하게 변화가 필요한 부분도 있고, 시간을 들여서 조금씩 바꿀 수 있는 부분도 있습니다. 중요한 것은 반덤핑관세와 상계관세를 비롯하여 트럼프 정부의 기존 무역정책을 수정해야 한다는 점입니다. 타국에 대한 환율조작국 지정이나 임의적인 상계관세 부과도 WTO 협정에 어긋납니다. 이 사안을 깊이 파고들자면 끝도 없지만, 요지는 타국이 자국에 유리한 방향으로 조작한다고 미국이 의심할 경우, 반덤핑이나 상계관세와 같이 교역을 왜곡하는 조치를 이행할 가능성이 있다는 점입니다. 특히 미국이 국가안보상 이유를 원용하며 취하는 무역왜곡 조치가 문제입니다. 미국은 자국의 자동차 산업을 보호하기 위해 일련의 조치를 이행했고, 향후에도 추가로 도입할 수 있다고 위협하고 있습니다.

WTO 체제의 발전이나 미국의 이익을 위해서라도 이 같은 보호무역주의는 긍정적이라 할 수 없습니다. 특히 트럼프 행정부는 무역정책 목표를 달성하는 데 있어 WTO를 사실상 외면하고 양자 협상에만 치중하는 모습입니다.

트럼프 대통령이 재선되면 세계무역체제는 중대한 위기에 빠질 것입니다. 미국이 계속해서 WTO 협정을 뒤흔들고 규칙을 위반하면 세계무역체제가 더 이상 버틸 수 없기 때문입니다. 미국의 압박을 느낀 다른 국가들도 일방적인 보호무역 정책을 펼칠 것이며, 이는 글로벌 무역 규칙에 균열을 초래할 것입니다.

민주당 후보가 당선되어도 문제입니다. 민주당은 트럼프 못지않게 중국의 무역정책에 부정적인 데다, 중국의 인권문제에 대해서는 더욱 강경한 입장입니다. 민주당 행정부가 중국의 인권을 문제 삼을 경우, 중국은 미국이 무역보복을 했을 때보다 더 강력하게 반발할 것입니다. 그러나 역내 및 다자차원의 협력이나 글로벌 경제기구의 강화에서는 민주당이 공화당보다 열린 자세를 보일 가능성이 높습니다. 제가 세계무역체제에 가지는 유일한 낙관적인 기대입니다.

한국은 국제 경제관계에서 자국에 주어진 선택지를 재검토해야 합니다. 정책 불확실성을 해소하기 위해 역내의 어떤 국가와 무역협정을 체결해야 하는지, 어떻게 투자와 기술이전을 활성화하여 경제적 자원의 효율적 활용을 촉진할 것인지 고민해야 합니다. 이를 통한 경제발전을 이루려면 대내적으로는 경제를 개혁하고, 대외적으로는 시장을 개방하여 타국이 한국에 수출과 투자를 할 수 있는 기회를 보장해야 합니다. 다른 자리에서도 비슷한 말씀을 드린 바 있지만, CPTPP(포괄적·점진적 환태평양 경제동반자 협정)의 추진이야말로 아시아 태평양 지역에서 미·중 협력을 촉진할 수 있는 발판이 될 것입니다.

세계무역체제를 굳이 낙관적으로 전망하자면 이 정도입니다. 제한시간을 넘어서 발표해서 죄송합니다. 한·일 갈등을 길게 다루다 보니 시간이 늦어졌습니다. 한국과 일본은 서로의 발전과 우호관계 증진을 위한 노력을 경주해야 할 것입니다. 경청해 주셔서 감사합니다.

미·중, 한·일 무역분쟁과 세계 무역체제의 미래

질의 응답

Q 강연 감사합니다. 저는 2개의 질문이 있습니다. 미국이 WTO를 외면하면서 다자 무역체제가 약화되었습니다. 한일 관계를 보면, 한국도 WTO 체제를 활용하고자 했지만 별 소득이 없었습니다. 그러나 미국이 중재한다면 한일 양국이 다시 대화에 나설 수도 있다고 봅니다. 문제는 미·중 갈등인데, 국가 간 갈등을 조율할 수 있는 상위 기구가 부재한 실정입니다. WTO의 개정이나, AIIB처럼 중국이 주도하는 완전히 새로운 기구의 등장에 대해 박사님께서는 가능성이 있다고 보십니까? AIIB와 WTO를 동일선상에서 비교할 수는 없겠지만요. 박사님의 견해는 어떠십니까?

A 저는 가능성이 없다고 봅니다. WTO 개정이라는 플랜 A가 실패한 지금 여러 플랜 B가 등장하고 있는데, 몇 년 전에는 TPP가 나왔습니다. 언젠가는 TPP 규정이 제네바의 다자무역체제에 이식될 것이라는 기대하에서요. 물론 쉬운 일은 아니지만, 적어도 미국이 TPP를 탈퇴하기 전에는 지금보다 상황이 나았습니다. 그러나 미국은 더 이상 TPP 회원국이 아닙니다. 그 결과 흥미로운 상황이 전개되었습니다.

다른 국가들은 여전히 TPP라는 플랫폼을 필요로 합니다. 일본, 호주, 뉴질랜드는 WTO 협정을 발전시킨 TPP 협정을 유지하며 이행 중입니다. 캐나다와 멕시코도 마찬가지입니다. 이 같은 무역규칙은 미·중 무역분쟁을 해결하는 기반이 될 수 있습니다. 단 그 이전에 미국과 중국이 대화를 해야 합니다. 향후 10년간 TPP 협정을 개정하여 미국과 중국의 참여를 유도하는 것도 방법입니다. 여러 TPP 국가들의 교역 파트너인 EU를 TPP에 끌어들

일 수도 있습니다. 이 경우 TPP 회원국들이 세계 GDP의 대부분을 차지하게 되고, TPP를 기초로 WTO 협정을 개정할 수 있습니다. 물론 그 과정에서 저소득 국가의 이해관계를 반영하는 조정 작업은 필요합니다. 지푸라기를 잡는 격이라고 할 수 있지만, 이만큼이라도 이루려면 한국이 지금보다 더 적극적으로 플랜 B를 검토해야 합니다.

Q 박사님의 강연 감사합니다. 저는 세계의 무역체제에 관해 질문이 있습니다. 지난 50년간 WTO 체제는 효과적으로 기능을 발휘했습니다. 그러나 트럼프 행정부는 WTO 체제에 반대하고 있으며, WTO 상소기구의 위원을 선출하는 것도 거부하는 중입니다. 현재 민주당 경선에서 사회주의자 2명이 선두주자인데, 이들 중 한 명이 대통령에 당선된다고 해도 기존의 무역질서를 수호하는 데 얼마나 적극적일지 의문입니다. 그 점에서 미국이 WTO에 부정적 모습을 유지할 경우 WTO 체제의 전망이 궁금합니다.

두 번째 질문입니다. 데이비드 리카도의 비교우위론이 등장한 이래 세계무역은 자유무역에 기초해 왔습니다. 교역 당사자 모두에게 이득이 되는 체제로 인식되었기 때문에, 누구도 그 효용성에 의문을 제기하지 않았습니다. 문제는 무역 과실의 배분 문제입니다. 이를 경제학에서는 충분히 다루지 않았습니다. 한국과 미국, 미국과 말레이시아 간의 교역에서는 이 같은 배분 문제가 크게 부각되지 않았습니다. 그러나 미·중 교역에서는 중대한 문제입니다. 또한 미·중 교역은 경제 문제를 넘어 지정학이나 패권경쟁의 요소를 지니고 있습니다. 지식인들은 트럼프가 정신 이상이라고 생각할 수도 있고, 그가 많은 비판을 받고 있는 것은 사실이지만, 미국인들은 트럼프를 지지하고 있습니다. 이에 대한 박사님의 견해가 궁금합니다. 감사합니다.

A 정확한 질문을 제대로 해주셨습니다. 저도 명확한 답변을 드리겠습니다. 먼저 WTO의 분쟁해결절차입니다. 효과적인 분쟁해결절차가 없다면 어떤 국가도 새로운 무역규칙 설정에 참여하지 않을 것입니다. 적용하지도 못할 규칙을 제정해봐야 의미가 없기 때문입니다. 아직은 미국이 WTO의 분쟁해결기구에서 탈퇴하지 않았습니다. 미국은 원하는 것은 분쟁해결절차의 폐지가 아닙니다. 미국에게 불리한 판결이 나올 수 있는 상소절차를 막는 것입니다.

올해 12월이 되면 라이트하이저 USTR 대표가 선호하는 결과가 나올 것입니다. 라이트하이저 대표는 효과적인 분쟁해결 절차를 원합니다. 분쟁해결기구에서 미국에게 유리한 판정이 나오면 기꺼이 승복하고, 불리한 판정이 나오면 상소하는 것입니다. 그러나 현재는 상소위원의 수가 정족수에 미치지 못하는 상태입니다. 상소기구에서 사건을 심리할 수 없기 때문에, 그 전단계인 원심 판정의 이행도 불가능합니다. 법적 공백이 발생하는 셈입니다. 미국에게 불리한 판정이 나와도 이를 이행할 수 있는 길이 막혔습니다. 동전 던지기에 비유하면, 앞 뒤 어느 면이 나오든 미국의 승리입니다. 바로 라이트하이저 대표가 가장 원하는 시나리오입니다. 미국이 WTO 협정을 위반해도 제재를 받을 일이 없기 때문입니다. 미국을 제외한 다른 국가들은 여전히 분쟁해결절차를 유지하고자 합니다. 기존의 상소기구를 대체하는 별도의 절차를 마련하여 미국이 당사자가 아닌 사건에 적용하려는 시도도 있습니다. 대체 절차가 도입된다고 해도 얼마나 지속될 수 있을지 의문입니다. 미국이 입장을 바꾸도록 설득할 수도 있겠지만, 이를 위해서는 미국에 그만한 대가를 지불해야 할 것입니다. 무역 협상의 전형적인 패턴에 따라 미국이 원하는 분야에서 다른 국가들이 양보하는 것입니다. 그 분야가 디지털 교역일 수도 있고, 다른 분야일 수도 있습니다. 그러나 현재로서는 WTO 협상은 라이트하이저 대표의 우선순위가 아닙니다.

두 번째도 아주 좋은 질문을 해주셨습니다. WTO가 지속가능한지와 관련하여 나오는 불평 중 하나가 교역에서 나오는 과실의 균등한 배분입니다. 각국 정부는 조세 정책이나 재정지출을 통해 무역의 혜택이 소득 수준에 상관없이 모두에게 돌아갈 수 있도록 해야 할 것입니다. 각 국가 수준을 넘어 국가 간 관계에서도 마찬가지입니다.

미국을 비롯한 여러 국가에서 상기의 배분 정책이 제대로 이행되지 않는 상황입니다. 민주당과 공화당 양측에서 기존의 무역질서에 대한 반발이 커지고 있습니다. 사회 정의에도 어긋나고, 국가 주권도 침해한다는 것입니다. 이 같은 인식을 바꿀 수 있는 단서를 지난 주의 한 사건에서 찾을 수 있습니다. 투표권조차 없는 젊은 청년들이 기후변화에 관심을 갖게 된 것입니다. 트럼프 행정부에서는 전혀 관심이 없는 주제입니다. 저는 USTR의 무역·환경 자문위원회의 의장을 맡은 바 있는데, 미국이 체결한 무역협정에서는 늘 환경에 관한 별도의 장을 포함시켰습니다. 오바마 행정부에서도 마찬가지였습니다. 반면 트럼프 행정부는 환경 정책에서 실패했습니다. 만일 민주당 후보가 당선된다면 환경 문제가 주요 국정과제가 될 것입니다. 여러 무역규칙을 통한 녹색성장 촉진이야말로 다시금 국제무역에 대한 광범위한 지지를 이끌어낼 수 있는 방법입니다. 그 혜택이 모든 계층에 고루 돌아가지 않을 수도 있습니다. 그러나 녹색 딜(Green Deal)을 이뤄내면, 젊은 층의 무역체제에 대한 관심을 일으키고 협력을 촉진하는 계기로 삼을 수 있다고 생각합니다.

이는 신중한 작업이 필요한 부분입니다. 그동안 환경정책에 대한 많은 연구가 이뤄졌습니다. 워렌 상원의원도 일련의 환경정책을 내놓았습니다. 이 정책들을 보면 목표는 잘 잡았지만, 세부적인 면에서 치명적인 오류가 있습니다. 국경간 탄소조정(Border Carbon Adjustment)를 비롯한 여러 정책 제안을 보면 실현가능성이 떨어집니다. 그러나 재생에너지를 활성화하고, 재생에너지 자원을 확대하기 위한 인프라 투자는 긍정적인 부분입니다. WTO 협정 초기 5년간 존재했던 단기 및 영구 보조금 정책을 재생에너지 산업에 시행하는 것도 검토할 가치가 있습니다. 향후 WTO가 발전하기 위해서는 WTO 목표의 방향을 재설정해야 합니다. 제가 WTO 체제에 거는 유일한 기대입니다.

Q 오늘의 조찬강연을 빌려 드리고 싶은 질문이 있습니다. 어제 트럼프 대통령과 아베 총리가 미일 FTA 협정을 타결했습니다. 두 정상은 서로에게 축하의 말을 건넸습니다. 물론 완전한 자유무역협정이라고 할 수는 없지만, 일본은 소고기와 농산물 시장을 개방했고 미국은 일본산 자동차 부품에 적용되는 관세를 인하하기로 약속했습니다. 저는 이 같은 자유화 조치를 서

비스 부문으로 확장하면 어떨까 생각했습니다. 그렇게 되면 TPP 11에 한국이나 미국이 가입할 수 있을 것입니다. 그러나 현재의 한일 갈등을 고려할 때 한국의 TPP 가입에 일본이 동의할지 궁금합니다. 박사님 견해는 어떠십니까?

A 이번 주에 타결된 미일 FTA는 미니딜(mini deal)이라고 할 수 있습니다. 이 협정은 두 단계로 이루어져 있습니다. 1단계에서는 현 TPP 수준의 농산물 시장에 대한 접근성을 일본이 미국에게 보장합니다. 무역특혜라기보다는 공정한 경쟁의 기회를 제공하는 것에 가깝습니다. 그 대가로 미국은 관세를 인하합니다. 의회의 동의 없이 대통령 권한으로 이행할 수 있는 비교적 낮은 폭의 관세 인하입니다. 5% 이하의 관세는 전면 철폐되고, 5% 이상의 관세는 절반까지 인하할 수 있습니다. 그러나 민감품목에 대해서는 이 같은 관세 인하가 적용되지 않는 것으로 알려졌습니다. 자동차도 마찬가지입니다.

미일 FTA는 내년 봄에 시작될 무역협상 본게임의 시작점에 불과합니다. 만일 이 협상이 성공적으로 끝난다면 TPP에 버금가는 협정을 이끌어낼 수 있을 것입니다. 그러나 라이트하이저 대표는 이번 주의 기자회견에서 "미국은 TPP 수준의 합의를 원한다. 그러나 TPP 수준의 양보를 할 수는 없다"고 밝혔습니다. 이번 협정에서 미국의 대차대조표를 보면, 미국이 상대로부터 받은 양보는 TPP 수준에 미치지 못합니다. 대신 미국이 상대에게 한 양보도 TPP보다는 낫습니다. 그러나 TPP를 나오고 대신 미일 FTA를 체결한 것이 그만한 가치가 있을까요? TPP 탈퇴로 인해 미국의 시장 점유율은 떨어졌습니다. 반면 TPP에 잔류한 유럽이나 호주를 비롯한 다른 국가들은 미국보다 일찍 일본시장을 선점할 수 있었습니다. 그 점을 감안하면 과연 TPP를 탈퇴할 필요가 있었는지 의문입니다. 이제 미일 FTA가 타결된 만큼 미국이 잃었던 시장 점유율을 즉시 회복할 수 있을까요? 결코 그런 일은 없을 겁니다. 기업인이라면 아시겠지만, 한 번 잃은 시장을 저절로 되찾을 수는 없습니다. 미국이 시장 점유율을 회복하려면 그만한 노력과 시간을 들여야 할 것입니다.

Jeffrey J. Schott

Mr. Schott is a senior fellow of working on international trade policy and economic sanctions at the Peterson Institute for International Economics (PIIE). Mr. Schott was also a visiting lecturer at Princeton University and an adjunct professor at Georgetown University. He worked as an official of the US Treasury Development in international trade and energy policy. He is a member of the State Department's Advisory Committee on International Economic Policy.

U.S.-China, Korea-Japan Trade Disputes and the Global Trading System

Jeffrey J. Schott
Senior Fellow
Peterson Institute for International Economics (PIIE)

Thank you very much Dr. Jun and Dr. SaKong. The relationship that my colleagues and I have had with your institute has been a long and fruitful one. It's a great honor to be invited back time and time again to join you and to engage in discussions with the very distinguished audience that you always gather.

Today you've given me a difficult task and a long title for my talk. U.S.-China, Korea-Japan trade disputes and the future of the world trading system. I think anyone could have taken one part of that title and spent an hour. But I have 30 minutes and I will try to integrate ideas and comments on all three, and hopefully put it in a way that inspires some questions about the issues that I've left out.

I'll start with the U.S.-China trade dispute which actually is a long-standing one. For the convenience of the talk, we will start the dispute since the introduction or the entry into office of President Trump in January 19, 2017.

The U.S.-China trade war was initially deemed to be and exercised in rebalancing trade. There were concerns about the very large merchandise trade imbalance though most economists would tell you that it was not a serious area of concern. But the idea was to propel more Chinese purchases of U.S. goods and to blunt Chinese subsidies and regulatory policies that distorted international trade and investment particularly in traditional industries. Steel was an immediate focus of the Trump administration. High-tech issues have followed subsequently.

Now what has been interesting and important to keep in mind is that players on both sides thought the conflict would be short and yield a modest array of Chinese commitments to remove discrimination against U.S. firms. But instead, after 5 or 6 quarters of conflict and volatile swings, which you can say manic and depressive almost on the turn of a tweet, you have movement towards an agreement as we had in April of this year. Then the deal suddenly unravels. And then it is brought back together again. The markets react gleefully and talks resume. And then another snag hits. And you enter into the manic depressive cycle again. That continues today. Now we're on a manic part of the phase with officials meeting and trying to put the trade negotiations back on track, with the hope that senior level officials will meet in Washington on October 10th and 11th to try to regain momentum for at least a preliminary agreement that will halt this cycle of tariff escalation.

It has come at costs. The prolonged fighting has setback prospects for U.S.-China economic cooperation going forward by increasing mistrust between the two sides. That has had spillover effects on relations with countries and the region particularly Korea and it has damaging implications for the World Trade Organization(WTO).

Let me just mention very briefly where we are in this fight right now. If threats that have been issued in the past month or two are fulfilled by December 15th, U.S. penalty tariffs will cover about 97% of imports from China with an average duty of about 24%. That's compared with an average most favored nation(MFN) duty of 3% before the start of the trade war.

This was a key promise of President Trump to his supporters during the 2016 campaign that he would impose tariffs on China's goods, make them more expensive in the U.S. market. He talked about 35 to 45% during the campaign. But he's essentially fulfilled his promise of raising tariffs almost 25% across the board on Chinese goods if there is the imposition of the threatened tariff increases on October 15th and on December 15th of this year. Almost all Chinese imports will be subject to very high penalty duties from 15 to 30%.

China has retaliated in kind but a little more carefully. Because policy makers in Beijing have been cautious about imposing costs on their own companies and when you tax imports you can tax local production. You certainly can tax exports that use imported components. So China has or will have by December 15th impose penalty tariffs on about 69% of U.S. exports, leaving out important sectors such as most aircraft and pharmaceuticals and the like, where there aren't easy substitutes or alternative suppliers, and where the U.S. goods are needed to maintain the competitiveness of Chinese productions.

Like the U.S., the average trade-weighted tariff will go up to about 25 to 26% from the MFN rate before the start of the tariff war of 8%. So a big price wedge between the price, the access of U.S. goods to the Chinese market compared to the access of other foreign goods to the Chinese market. To further exacerbate that discrimination or that price discrimination, China has engaged in a reduction of MFN tariffs on many goods, for everybody else. So the discrimination against U.S. exporters is actually bigger than the 26% because the MFN tariff has gone down for other countries just as the tariff applied to U.S. goods has gone up.

In some sectors, this has made a tremendous difference with a tariff differential of 25% or more. That has encouraged significant diversion away from U.S. exports in agriculture and soybeans for example, but also in other products. The U.S. tariffs have also caused trade diversion away from Chinese exporters but it hasn't gone back to U.S. production. The main effect of the tariff war and that in the dislocation of Chinese exports to the U.S. has been the shifting of goods to other exporters in East and Southeast Asia.

What we've seen so far is basically China has raised tariffs on U.S. goods and has lowered tariffs on everyone else as a result of the actions of both the U.S. and China increased protectionism on both sides. U.S.-China trade exports and imports have gone down. U.S. trade deficit with China has gone down slightly though a very small dent in a very large bilateral merchandise and deficit. Trade diversion has increased with some U.S. imports sourced out of Southeast Asia instead of China. The global U.S. trade deficit has been about the same. It's actually slightly higher. Less due to that the tariff war then to the fact that the U.S. economy has been relatively robust and the dollar has appreciated. That has led to a very large U.S. merchandise trade deficit.

In that sense the trade war doesn't seem to have been worth all the damage that's been done so far with one exception. President Trump made one of his promises that he would raise tariffs and he has done that. He regards this as a key promise upheld to his supporters who he depends on to maintain their strict loyalty to him in the 2020 presidential election. So there is an economic component. There is a political component. As we get closer and closer to the election next November 2020, politics will dominate economic considerations.

There is an attempt to reach an agreement as negotiators are working on a preliminary agreement to at least have a ceasefire in the U.S.-China trade war and in the escalation of the tariffs. China adds to that purchases of U.S. goods and makes commitments on foreign investment and intellectual property, which they can do, based on laws they have already promulgated and that will enter into force in January of next year. They can even elaborate a little bit on the foreign investment issues and the protection of intellectual property in China.

That type of an agreement is unlikely to be sustained amid the political pressure from both Republicans and Democrats to challenge China and to say that any deal that Trump made with China has been too soft as part of the political debate leading up to the election. That leads me to think that any deal that could arise, that hopefully will arise in the coming weeks or months, which would partially rollback some of tariff increases, or prevent the additional tariff increases that are scheduled in the coming 2 months.

However, I significantly doubt that type of deal can be sustained. We'll be back into a period of disruption just as the uncertainty increases in the U.S. political debate next year.

So far, the net effect of the increased tariffs has been a small decline in GDP in both the U.S. and China. These are two very large economies. Even though there's 500 billion dollars of imports by the U.S. from China, you raise that cost by 25%, you're still only talking about 125 billion dollars which for an economy, over 20 trillion dollars. That's still relatively small in macro terms.

That leads some people to say "Well... don't worry about it. It's just tariffs". The problem is it's not just tariffs. As many businessmen in the room know what the more damaging factor in the tariff war has been the increased uncertainty, the lack of policy predictability that makes it much more difficult to make investment decisions. That has led some investors to sit on their hands and forego new investments that are needed to promote and propel economic growth. It has led others by necessity because of the threat to their supply chains, to engage in relatively less efficient investment whether it'd be in excess inventories or redundant supplier relationships, supply chains. One supplier is blocked because of new policy sanctions.

This is inefficient. It reduces productivity and it is built into the system and it will constrain economic growth over the medium term. So the damage that you're seeing on the investment front, it's much more serious than the immediate damage that you're seeing on the tariff front. That applies not only to the U.S. and China but to all the other economies affected who do business with them and also suffer from the same uncertainty in global economic prospects.

This is, I think, a part of the U.S. strategy that was not well-prepared, and is damaging U.S. and Chinese interests. For the U.S., I think it has a near-term prospect because we're facing an election next year. And the political prospects while the U.S. economy is weakening, I think, will be a factor in the decision on who is the elected president next year.

Normally, incumbent presidents have a great advantage in being reelected, especially if the economy is doing well. So President Trump is going to try to do everything he can to keep modest but reasonable economic growth. The employment situation is very good. Interest rates are low and so if he could keep economic conditions the way they are today, he'd stand a good chance of being re-elected. I will abstract from the developments of the last two days on that I can talk about that later. I'm talking about economics here. But the likelihood is that there will be softening economic growth. That's why President Trump is putting so much pressure on the Fed. But there is a very low likelihood that the Fed will accommodate the President's demands, which are for very large additional cuts in interest rates.

There's another factor to the U.S.-China trade war that is causing problems and that is much harder to resolve and will be much more long-standing. That is the friction on high-technology trade and investment. It is one that goes beyond disputes about Huawei and ZTE. It is rooted in concern about technological competition. It is rooted in concern about the misappropriation of technology through cyber security intrusions. It has led to legislation promulgated in 2018. That severely increases the screening of foreign direct investment in the U.S. particularly in high technology sectors.

The threat of that screening has already had a profound effect on Chinese foreign direct investment in the U.S. It's virtually dried up. The other overseas investment in the U.S., I think, is still maintained but companies are becoming more cautious because of the threat of screening in China and more because of the weakening economy and shifts in consumer preferences and in automobiles and other sectors. This also has an effect though on an outflow from the U.S. along with the increased screening of inward investment into the U.S. The Congress passed the Export Control Reform Act which increases controls on sensitive high-technology products and technologies that can be exported in two countries and end up in China. So it doesn't have to just involve the direct transfers of products to China. But it can involve the interruption or the tougher screening of contracts between the U.S. and Korea and the U.S. and Japan for fear that there would then be a diversion of the technology or the product to China.

This is something that could get very severe, depending on how the U.S. government defines which it is now doing in the context of implementing regulations for last year's legislation, defining what is an emerging and foundational technology.

Now if you don't know what that means, you're in good company. Neither does the U.S. government and neither do I. But it's a lot more than what you've screening so far and controlling so far. And how extensive the definition is will depend on how restrictive U.S. surveillances on outflows of high-tech goods and technologies.

This is a problem that is complicated. It is generating very strong political reactions in both the U.S. and China. It's become more than an economic issue. It's a national security issue and it is led to a sharp, negative reaction in Beijing, just as it's generated strong antagonistic feelings in the U.S. Congress against China.

This is something that's not going to be resolved by trade negotiators and is going to be a part of the landscape of Asia-Pacific economic relations even if we find a way accommodating the trade disputes.

There's the third area of potential increase in U.S.-China relations and that involves the U.S. economic sanctions against Iran, North Korea and Venezuela. Particularly the oil sanctions against Iran and Venezuela. The U.S. has pursued a policy of trying to squeeze, very tightly, revenues generated from oil and gas exports from Iran and Venezuela. China is the main oil customer of those countries. Since May, any company buying oil or gas, shipping those products, financing those products whether it's a barter transaction or a debt relief payment, any of those energy companies, shipping companies, financial institutions are liable to very serious U.S. economic sanctions, leading to basically disbarment from markets using U.S. dollars. Which means basically you can't do business outside and for most of the world economy.

In China, one has to suspect strongly and I am sure U.S. intelligence agencies have the proof that the main state-owned energy companies, Sinopec and China National Petroleum Company, are involved in those transactions along with major financial institutions. If sanctions are imposed against those companies, then the U.S.-China trade dispute is elevated to a different level. Very disruptive. It doesn't make any sense to do that. So far the administration has been very careful. Because China is cooperating with policy on Iran and North Korea to an extent, it's reduced to the extent that it benefits China. With regard to Iran, China has had to reduce its purchases but it's used the leverage of the U.S. sanctions to get better prices. So Iran has to deeply discount the price that it sells oil to China to maintain those flows.

However, if the White House decides that it wants to escalate and really cause a dust up, it can happen. And soon after I wrote a piece about this, there was an announcement from the U.S. Treasury Department that additional Chinese ships were being sanctioned this week, just a few days ago, for dealing in Iranian crude. I can talk about that if you like, but there are some potential major areas of disruption that need to be avoided, as I said in my piece, to prevent from throwing oil onto the existing fire of U.S.-China trade disputes.

As I feared I'm spending too much time and I need to say a few words about the Korea-Japan dispute. Not entirely unrelated, because Japan and Korea are also victims of the U.S.-China trade war and the disruptions to the supply chains.

If you were a businessman or someone worried about economic growth in Korea, you wouldn't take steps to further exacerbate the problems that economic forces in your own economy needed to be dealt with because of the disruption from U.S.-China. You would think that there would be a way of managing a long-standing political, diplomatic, cultural dispute that with an economic partner who accounts for, less than 10% of total merchandise trade, but importantly concentrated in key sectors of the Korean economy.

And Japan as well has a much more dominant position in terms of foreign investment in the Korean economy, almost 50 billion dollars of investment, accounting more than 20% of foreign direct investment in Korea. That's divided about half and half between manufacturing and services. But it's still you know when you get to 50 billion dollars, it's a significant impact on the economy.

Now I'm not here to preach about the cause of the Korean-Japan dispute. You all know that better than me, but I can sympathize with the concerns. My own family suffered during the war terribly in concentration camps, and some were exterminated. However, it is up to the political leaders of countries to deal with these long-standing problems and manage their effects, so that they minimize the damage to each society. That is not being done in my view, and there are

3 governments to blame. Three. Japan and Korea, the dispute is undermining their own national security interests, and those of the U.S. Economic Security is being compromised as well, threatening further damage to supply chains already adversely affected by the U.S.-China trade war. There is no credible economic rationale for discriminating against the traded goods of each other, for national security reasons.

There's been a lot of litigation in the WTO. That's fine but both sides are vulnerable to losing that litigation in the WTO, under existing WTO rules. That's the decision that's going to take months and months, probably years to resolve and the damage is proceeding now. So WTO litigation is not going to factor importantly in the resolution or the management of this problem.

Long standing problems should not impair urgently needed bilateral cooperation in the face of common security threats in the region. This is critical. I know there are a lot of factors involved in the policies that have been taken by President Moon and Prime Minister Abe. As an American I can say, that's unfortunate and it's counterproductive. I don't pass judgement on either. But I will pass judgement on my own government. Even worse than the actions taken by the U.S. allies is the inaction of the Trump administration. Allowing the fracturing of a critical U.S. Security Alliance is one of the most profound failures of the Trump administration to date.

I've been in Washington for almost 50 years. I can't

imagine instance where a U.S. President would not be actively engaged and sitting down with key allies and working out a way of managing their differences, so that it would not impair our common security interests. And yet, while we have representatives from the State Department here in town, the comments are so milk-toast. This is a critical problem for the U.S. security and it should be recognized as such. However, we're not doing enough.

The security issue dominates the economics. But when Korea and Japan are divided and the U.S. is not engaged, then the ability to manage the economic fallout from the U.S.-China dispute become more limited. It is harder or it closes off options for cooperation or for efforts that Korea can take to use trade and investment in the region, to compensate or offset some of the adverse effects of the U.S.-China trade war. I don't think that's a sufficiently accepted or understood in Seoul, in Tokyo or in Washington, at least judged by the reactions to date.

I say this as a longtime friend of Korea, as someone who worked very hard 20 years ago to ensure the strengthening of our alliance, economic and security, through the Korea-U.S. free trade agreement. I've been a promoter of that and a friendship between our countries. Similarly, with Japan, we need to have a security relationship that is so close that there's no light between it. We have to be careful about anything that risks even moving up apart a little. I think there's a lot of responsibility in Washington to do more.

That leads me to the last part of my charge this afternoon and that is you're wondering how I was going to pull all of these together. I'm trying to figure that out myself.

What does this mean for the global trading system? So far it's bad for the trading system. Because what the U.S. is doing to China and what China has retaliated in kind, is illegal under the WTO rules. That is not helping to establish trust in a forum that could moderate the dispute or serve as a foundation for resolution. We're not taking sufficient steps to work with our allies, to try to find broader regional or multilateral responses to the problems raised by the U.S.-China dispute. We're attacking the very countries that we need to be working with us and undercutting the multilateral system the WTO that would be the area where we have the opportunity to work with China.

This dispute has put the WTO in some jeopardy and rules-based international trading system in crisis and at risk, because we are undercutting the basis for going back to negotiating table and updating the international trade rulebook. If you think about it with only a small exception, the world trading rulebook was developed in the early 1990s and hasn't been changed since, while world trade has changed dramatically since then. As a result, the WTO has been notably unsuccessful in updating the rulebook and we've had to look outside of the WTO to regional agreements starting. The KORUS FTA was a big upgrade in many areas over WTO rules and providing precedents for the multilateral trading system if and when negotiations at the multilateral level, at the global level could proceed. The Trans-Pacific Partnership(TPP) adopted most of the KORUS FTA. It was basically modeled after the KORUS FTA to spread those disciplines to major countries in the Asia Pacific region based on American values and American trade and economic practices. That's what President Trump withdrew from and since that time, to be perfectly honest, he has spent most of his trade policy efforts trying to undo the damage that he did on day three of his administration. The agreement in North America with Canada and Mexico is largely a reiteration of TPP with some additional auto-protection thrown in. The deal that was just announced with Japan reconstructs the agricultural deal, with a little less than what the U.S. would have gotten in the TPP, but without major U.S. concessions in other areas. The KORUS FTA, after a lot of dispute, was left virtually intact, with changes that did not have major commercial significance but at the payment of steel quotas that cut Korean steel exports to the U.S. by over a third.

We're seeing this increased protectionism which goes against what the WTO is supposed to prevent. The problem is, in the U.S.-China context, that we're dealing with, not China not playing by the rules, because largely China is playing by rules and when it hasn't, the U.S. has brought them to the WTO. We've won almost all of those cases, except a few dealing with anti-dumping practices that are particularly irksome to our Ambassador Lighthizer.

The biggest problem is that China has policies that distort trade and investment, that are either bending the rules a little, or basically circumventing the rules, or entering territory where the WTO has ambiguous rules, or no rules at all. That has only underscored the damage that is being done to the world trading system by not having successful multilateral negotiations that constantly upgraded the rulebook. The cost of the failure of The Doha Round is now being basically exhibited, demonstrated in many new trade disputes including the U.S.-China trade war.

Fixing the WTO requires cooperation and participation by the major trading countries. This is where I tie everything together. You're not going to get acceptance in the WTO of new international rules, unless the U.S. and China cooperate with each other, and unless Korea and Japan, and other major trading nations are a part of the process of developing those rules. Having the U.S. and China increasing their mistrust of each other, and having Japan and Korea increasing their mistrust each other, only makes it more and more difficult to move forward at the regional or multilateral level. Updating the rulebook will require changing policies or current national positions in key areas. Some of which would need to be done sooner rather than later but some could be phased in over time. But it also will require changes in what the U.S. has been doing, particularly since the advent of Trump administration with regard to anti-dumping and countervailing duties. Some changes in domestic U.S. law which are dealing with currency manipulation and basically adding provisions to U.S. countervailing duty law that will be violations of the WTO. That's getting pretty deep in the weeds, but essentially the concern about currency manipulation is going to lead to more U.S. distortions through the use of anti-dumping and countervailing duties. Of course most prominently, the abuse of national security provisions which the U.S. has done to increasing extent and threatens to do in the auto sector.

This does not cast an optimistic forecast for moving forward in the WTO and it does not provide a good means for the current administration to move forward, because they've shown very little interest in using the WTO to promote their negotiating objectives, relying almost primarily on bilateral negotiations.

I think if President Trump is reelected, we will have a serious crisis in the world trading system, because the trading rules can't really withstand more abuse and lack of enforcement. There will be more and more pressure in the U.S. and other countries to act unilaterally and follow the example of the Trump administration. That will lead to a fracturing of the trading rules.

I think if a democrat is elected, there will still be major

challenges because the democrats are as critical of China as President Trump and will be even more critical of Chinese practices with regard to human rights which will have an even stronger reaction in Beijing than some of the initiatives of the Trump administration. However, the Democrats probably would be more open to working closely with Korea and Japan if there was a workable process to try to find regional and multilateral solutions and to strengthen international economic institutions. And I think that is my sole ray of optimism going forward.

What this means for Korea is to re-evaluate the options you have for international economic relations particularly in the region, what needs to be done with whom, how to work out agreements, that will increase policy predictability and help promote the more efficient use of economic resources, inflow of investment and technology to strengthen the Korean economy. That's something which requires some planning, both in terms of domestic economic reform and in terms of working with trading partners to ensure open access and opportunities for export and investment in major trading partners, China, Japan and elsewhere. I've said it on this platform many times before but a re-evaluation of the CPTPP would be an order at that stage including pushing the U.S. and China to work towards building a bridge using that Asia-Pacific initiative.

That's about as optimistic as I can get to Mr. Chairman

and I apologize for running over on my time but I got carried away on the Korea-Japan issue. I am sincerely and personally on that and in the spirit of trying to help friends find a way of making things better for their own economy in their own society. Thank you very much.

U.S.–China, Korea–Japan Trade Disputes and the Global Trading System

Questions and Answers

Q Thanks Jeffrey once again. I have two questions. As you pointed out, the WTO are getting weaker as U.S. really ditches the scene and then also in a way, you know about Korea-Japan situation also, we tried to leverage the WTO, but it seems to be fairly dysfunctional in a way. But to the extent that the U.S. still can mediate between two countries to probably have a better conversation, I think we are hopeful on that, but then when there is a really growing tension between China and the U.S. and there's no bigger omnipotent governing bodies out there. Do you think there is a chance that we might see another rise of new version of the WTO or maybe like AIIB? Maybe not the best comparison but do you think a totally new organization led by Chinese regime be possible? Do you think there will be a chance?

A I don't think so. What you can see is an evolving plan B and a few years ago that was the TPP, as a way of moving forward with upgrading the rules, so that it could be then transported back to Geneva to a broader multilateral. That was always difficult but it was easier when the U.S. was in it. With the U.S. leaving, it actually has created an interesting dynamic.

Other countries need to have that platform maintained. So Japan and Australia and New Zealand have kept the updated rulebook in place and are implementing it. Canada and Mexico are doing it as well. It's the type of rules that you want to at least have as the basis for dealing with the problems between the U.S. and China. But it means getting the U.S. and China back to engaging with each other. And maybe even over time, the next decade, by modifying the TPP, it can accommodate the participation of those countries. The European Union with trade ties with many of the TPP countries would be an additional participant. But once you do that, you've basically have most of the world's GDP at the table and then you can find the basis for bringing it back to Geneva so that it can apply for all countries and deal with the particular adjustment or problems of the poorer countries. That's grasping at straws perhaps, but it does require a more positive view towards the regional plan B than Korea has been willing to consider today.

Q Thank you Jeff. I would like to continue on the question of the overall trade regime. The WTO has been effective for the last half century, but President Trump is pretty much against it, and apparently declining to appoint a Member of Appellate Body. Furthermore, even if Democrats to displace him with two socialists as a front runner in the Democratic Party, I don't know how much interested they are in maintaining the system. I would like to ask your opinion of the future regime of the WTO and if U.S. does not actively participate, can there be any effective global trade panel.

I would like to add one more question. Ever since David Ricardo, international trade always believed in free trades. Nobody questioned it because both parties benefit out of it. But the one question that the economists did not address is how is that benefit shared. Now that did not matter as long as it was like the U.S. and Korea or the U.S. and Malaysia or etc. But when it comes to the U.S. and China, this becomes a very serious problem. And then to add it furthermore, one thing that international economy did not address is they saw the economic issue but not the impact of geopolitical, hegemonic relationship. Although President Trump looks insane to a lot of intellect and a lot of ranking profiles, Americans do support his attitudes. How do you address that? Thank you.

A I think you've put both those questions very precisely and very correctly. I will give you clear responses. On dispute settlement, it is necessary to have an effective system of dispute settlement in the WTO. Otherwise you can't guarantee the enforcement of the rules and no one will negotiate new rules. Why would you negotiate new rules if you can't enforce? The U.S. has not dropped out of the dispute settlement system. It wants to avoid the appellate process for cases that goes against the U.S.

The situation that will evolve in December of this year is exactly what Ambassador Lighthizer wants. He wants an effective panel decision process and if the ruling favors the U.S., great. We applaud it. If the ruling goes against the U.S., we appeal. But since there is no one to hear the appeal or you can't construct a panel, under WTO rules the initial ruling cannot be implemented. It goes into judicial limbo until the appellate process is complete. So essentially the ruling against the U.S. is blocked. How I describe it is, you're flipping a coin. Heads I win, tails you lose. That's the perfect scenario for Ambassador Lighthizer. It means that the U.S. is basically not held accountable when it's in violation. Everyone else is under the dispute settlement process and other countries are working out surrogate appellate procedures that would apply to disputes among themselves, but not when they are in dispute with the U.S. That's not going to be a sustainable situation. I think that you can get a change in the U.S. position but countries will have to pay for it, in typical trade negotiating fashion by making concessions in other areas to what the U.S. wants. Maybe it's on digital trade, maybe it's on other substantive areas that depends. But right now, negotiating in the WTO is not a priority for Ambassador Lighthizer.

Your second point is also very perceptive. Part of the problem of sustaining support for the WTO is complaints about the inequitable sharing of benefits. Both between countries rich and poor, and among countries, which is the responsibility of each government on how it adjusts its tax and expenditure policies to distribute the gains from trade.

Many countries including my own do a terrible job at that. There's built up resistance in both the Democrats and the Republicans to the existing system of trading rules either on social equity grounds or on sovereignty grounds. There is a way of beginning to change that debate. I think you heard some resonance of it the past week. Mostly from very young people, many who were not old enough to vote, who are talking about climate change. That's an issue that is not being considered at all by the Trump administration. I chaired the trade and environment policy advisory committee to USTR when they were doing a good job on environment chapters in their trade agreements. Obama administration did as well. They have dropped the ball on climate change. If a Democrat is elected, that will be one of the priority areas of concern. Developing a system that promotes a green economy through various trade rules could be a way of reviving broader-based support for international trade negotiations. But it would have a different payoff to different segments of the society. And the Green Deal, I think brings in the younger generations that would see renewed interest and opportunity in working with the trading system.

This is something that requires a lot of careful work. There have been some studies and proposals put forward by Senator Warren and others that are essentially have good objectives but are fatally flawed in their detail, talking about Border Carbon Adjustment taxed and other types of policies that would be difficult to implement. But the green areas – promoting renewables, promoting investment in infrastructure to support the expansion of renewable energy resources and providing exemptions short-term or permanent for subsidies to promote that type of development in societies as existed in the WTO in its first 5 years – are all things that deserve a lot more attention. In my view, if there's any hope for the WTO in the next decade, it will be through this reorientation of the WTO agenda and working in that way. I hope so because this is one of the last gasp of optimism that I have for the trading system.

Q I want to explore this issue a little bit further. Yesterday President Trump and Prime Minister Abe Shinzo, they congratulated each other to reach a U.S.-Japan trade deal. We are not calling it a free trade but nevertheless Japan opened up its beef sector and agricultural products and also U.S. lowered the tariff on the auto part and so on. So I thought if Japan and U.S. expand the sectoral coverage including service, that is nothing but the U.S.-Japan free trade which will open the entry to scrapped TPP. Once that happens maybe Korea should join the current TPP 11 together with the U.S. But given the ongoing conflict between Korea and Japan, I wonder if Japan would be willing to accept Korea's attempt to enter expanded TPP going back to original status. What is your view on this?

A The agreement that was announced this week is really a mini deal. It is intended to be the first stage of a 2-stage process. Basically, the first stage is increasing agriculture access to levels comparable to those existing for current TPP members. Not preferences but leveling the playing field. In return, the U.S. had some relatively minor tariff cuts that can be done under existing tariff cutting authority which you don't have to go to the Congress to get approval. Some of the tariffs can be eliminated if they're under 5%, some of the tariffs can be cut by 50%, if they're over 5%. But no sensitive products I believe are included and automobiles are not included.

This is just a down payment on a real free trade agreement that would be negotiated only starting in the spring of next year. If that could be concluded, one would expect a deal very comparable to what was in the TPP. But as Ambassador Lighthizer said this week to the press, he said "We want something comparable to what we got in the TPP but we want to pay less." What they've achieved so far from what I can see is they've gotten something a bit less than the TPP and they've paid a bit less than they paid in the TPP. But was it worth all of the aggravation and the loss market share and the first mover advantages that Europe and Australia and other countries have in the Japanese market compared to U.S. exporters? Probably not. Does it mean that the U.S. suddenly recoups its market share? Absolutely not. As anyone who's in business knows, once you give up a market, you don't automatically get it back. You have to work to get it back and it's going to take sometimes to do that.

세계경제연구원 출간물 및
특별강연 시리즈 목록

IGE Publications

Occasional Paper Series

1993

	Title	Author
93-01	Clintonomics and the New World Order: Implications for Korea-US Relations	C. Fred Bergsten
93-02	The Uruguay Round, NAFTA and US-Korea Economic Relations	Jeffrey Schott

1994

	Title	Author
94-01	Korea in the World: Today and Tomorrow	Paul Kennedy
94-02	US-Japan Technological Competition and Implications for Korea	Ronald A. Morse
94-03	The Problems of the Japanese Economy and their Implications for Korea	Toyoo Gyohten
94-04	Changing US and World Economies and their Market Prospects	Allen Sinai
94-05	Prospects for New World Monetary System and Implications for Korea	John Williamson
94-06	The Promises of the WTO for the Trading Community	Arthur Dunkel

1995

	Title	Author
95-01	Mexican Peso Crisis and its Implications for the Global Financial Market	Charles Dallara
95-02	The World Economic Trend and US Economic Outlook	Allen Sinai
95-03	New Games, New Rules, and New Strategies	Lester Thurow
95-04	The United States and North Korea Future Prospects	Robert Scalapino
95-05	US Foreign Policy toward East Asia and the Korean Peninsula	James A. Baker III
95-06	US Trade Tension with Japan and their Implications for Korea	Anne O. Krueger
95-07	Prospects for Northeast Asian Economic Development: Japan's Perspective	Hisao Kanamori

1996

	Title	Author
96-01	Trends of International Financial Market and Prospects of Global Economy in 1996	Allen Sinai
96-02	Future European Model: Economic Internationalization and Cultural Decentralization	Jørgen Ørstrøm Møller
96-03	Evolving Role of the OECD in the Global Economy	Donald Johnston
96-04	The Political Context and Consequences of East Asian Economic Growth	Francis Fukuyama
96-05	Korea's New Global Responsibilities	A. W. Clausen

1997

	Title	Author
97-01	East Asia in Overdrive: Multinationals and East Asian Integration	Wendy Dobson
97-02	American Security Policy in the Asia Pacific - Three Crisis and How We Dealt with Them	William Perry
97-03	Public Sector Reform in New Zealand and its Relevance to Korea	Donald Hunn

1998

	Title	Author
98-01	Global Cooperations and National Government: Why We Need Multilateral Agreement on Investment	Edward Graham
98-02	Korean-American Relations: The Search for Stability at a Time of Change	W. Anthony Lake
98-03	Korea: From Vortex to Hub of Northeast Asia	Donald P. Gregg
98-04	German Unification: Economic Consequences and Policy Lessons	Juergen B. Donges
98-05	Globalization and versus Tribalization: The Dilemma at the End of the 20th Century	Guy Sorman

1999

	Title	Author
99-01	Economic and Political Situation in North Korea and Security in Northeast Asia	Marcus Noland
99-02	The International Financial Market and the US Dollar/Yen Exchange Rate: An Overview and Prospects for the Future	Kenneth S. Courtis

	Title	Author
99-03	Prospects and Policy Recommendations for the Korean Economy and Other Asian Economies	Donald Johnston/ Hubert Neiss
99-04	Reflections on Contrasting Present-day US and Japanese Economic Performances	Hugh Patrick
99-05	Challenge for the World Economy: Where Do the Risks Lie?	Rudiger Dornbusch

2000

	Title	Author
00-01	North Korea-US Relationship: Its Current Condition and Future Prospects	Stephen W. Bosworth
00-02	Global New Economy: Challenges and Opportunities for Korea	Soogil Young
00-03	Global Trend in Financial Supervision	YongKeun Lee
00-04	Asia Grows, Japan Slows: Prospects for the World Economy and Markets	Kenneth S. Courtis
00-05	The Future of International Financial System and its Implications for Korea	Morris Goldstein
00-06	Prospects for Millennium Round Trade Negotiations and Korea-US Free Trade Agreement	Jeffrey Schott/ InBeom Choi
00-07	Prospects for the Multilateral Economic Institutions	Anne O. Krueger
00-08	Avoiding Apocalypse: The Future of the Two Koreas	Marcus Noland
00-09	Attracting FDI in the Knowledge Era	Andrew Fraser
00-10	The Economic and Foreign Policies of the New US Administration and Congress	C. Fred Bergsten
00-11	Korea and the US: Partners in Prosperity and Security	Stephen W. Bosworth
00-12	The Outlook for Asia and Other Emerging Markets in 2000	Charles Dallara/ Robert Hormats
00-13	Relationship between Corporation and Finance: Current Status and Prospects	Youngkeun Lee
00-14	How Should Korea Cope with Financial Globalization	James P. Rooney

2001

	Title	Author
01-01	The US Economy on the Brink? Japan on the Edge? Implications for Korea	Kenneth S. Courtis
01-02	The Economic Policy of the Bush Administration toward Korea	Marcus Noland

	Title	Author
01-03	Overcoming 3Cs	Jeffrey D. Jones
01-04	High Tech, The Consequences for our Relationship with Technology on our Lives and Businesses	John Naisbitt
01-05	Korea and the IMF	Stanley Fischer
01-06	The Status of Korea's Restructuring: An Outlook over the Next 10 Years	Dominic Barton
01-07	The World Dollar Standard and the East Asian Exchange Rate Dilemma	Ronald McKinnon
01-08	Europe's Role in Global Governance and Challenges to East Asia	Pierre Jacquet

2002

	Title	Author
02-01	Managing Capital Inflows: The Chilean Experience	Carlos Massad
02-02	Globalization and Korea: Opportunities and Backlash and Challenges	Martin Wolf
02-03	The US-Japan Economic Relationship and Implications for Korea	Marcus Noland
02-04	US Global Recovery: For Real? - Prospects and Risks	Allen Sinai
02-05	Globalization: A Force for Good	Patricia Hewitt
02-06	The World after 9/11: A Clash of Civilization?	Francis Fukuyama
02-07	Hanging Together: On Monetary and Financial Cooperation in Asia	Barry Eichengreen
02-08	The Global Economy Rebounds - But How Fast and For How Long? Issues and Implications for Korea and Asia	Kenneth S. Courtis
02-09	The US Economy and the Future of the Dollar: An Outlook for the World Economy	Marcus Noland
02-10	The Doha Round: Objectives, Problems and Prospects	Jagdish Bhagwati
02-11	The Outlook for Korea and the Global Economy 2002-2003	Paul F. Gruenwald
02-12	The US and World Economy: Current Status and Prospects	John B. Taylor
02-13	9/11 and the US Approach to the Korean Peninsula	Thomas C. Hubbard
02-14	The Outlook for US Economy, the Dollar and US Trade Policy	C. Fred Bergsten
02-15	New Challenges and Opportunities for the Global Telecommunications and Information Industries	Peter F. Cowhey

2003

	Title	Author
03-01	The US and World Economy: After the Iraq War	Allen Sinai
03-02	Korea in the OECD Family	Donald Johnston
03-03	The New Role of the US in the Asia-Pacific	Charles Morrison
03-04	The Global Economic Outlook and the Impact of President Bush's Economic Stimulus Package	Phil Gramm
03-05	Europe and Germany in Transition, Where Will the Economies Go?	Hans Tietmeyer
03-06	Regional Financial Cooperation in East Asia	Eisuke Sakakibara
03-07	The Global Exchange Rate Regime and Implications for East Asian Currencies	John Williamson

2004

	Title	Author
04-01	General Outlook on the US and World Economy in 2004	Allen Sinai
04-02	Korea after Kim Jong-il	Marcus Noland
04-03	US-Japan Relations and Implications for Korea	Hugh Patrick/ Gerald Curtis
04-04	China's Economic Rise and New Regional Growth Paradigm	Zhang Yunling
04-05	The Case for a Common Currency in Asia	Robert Mundell
04-06	A Foreign Businessman's Observations on Korean Economy and Other Things	William C. Oberlin

2005

	Title	Author
05-01	US Trade Policy after the 2004 US Election	Peter F. Cowhey
05-02	Asia in Transition and Implications for Korea	Dominic Barton
05-03	Post-Election US and Global Economies: Market Prospects, Risks, and Issues	Allen Sinai
05-04	The Korean Economy: A Critical Assessment from the Japanese Perspective	Yukiko Fukagawa
05-05	The Blind Man and the Elephant: Competing Perspectives on Global Imbalances	Barry Eichengreen
05-06	Mutual Interdependence: Asia and the World Economy	Anne O. Krueger

	Title	Author
05-07	The Impact of China and India on the Global Economy	Wendy Dobson
05-08	Economic Integration between East Asia and Asia-Pacific	Robert Scollay
05-09	Moody's Perspective on Korea's Ratings	Thomas Byrne

2006

	Title	Author
06-01	Oil Prices, Ben Bernanke, Inflation, and the Fourth Energy Recession	Philip K. Verleger
06-02	US and Global Economy and Financial Market Prospects: Picking up Steam	Allen Sinai
06-03	Korea-US FTA: A Path to Sustainable Growth	Alexander Vershbow
06-04	Japan's Foreign Policy for Economy and Japan-Korea FTA	Oshima Shotaro
06-05	Japan's Economic Recovery: Implications for Korea	Yukiko Fukagawa
06-06	M&A in the 21st Century and its Implications	Robert F. Bruner
06-07	Korea's Growing Stature in the Global Economy	Charles Dallara
06-08	Asian Economic Integration and Common Asian Currency	Eisuke Sakakibara
06-09	Measuring American Power in Today's Complex World and China "Rising": What Lessons for Today from the Past?	Paul Kennedy/ Bernard Gordon
06-10	- Whither China? - The Global Scramble for IT Leadership: Winners and Losers	- Richard N. Cooper - George Scalise

2007

	Title	Author
07-01	Korea and the United States - Forging a Partnership for the Future: A View from Washington	Edwin J. Feulner
07-02	Germany: Understanding for the Underperformance since Reunification	Juergen B. Donges
07-03	Seismic Shifts, the World Economy, and Financial Markets in 2007	Allen Sinai
07-04	Changing Economic Environment: Their Implications for Korea	Angel Gurría
07-05	The Feasibility of Establishing an East Asian FTA: A Chinese Perspective	Zhang Yunling
07-06	The Global Oil and Gas Market: Paradigm Shift and Implications for Korea	Fereidun Fesharaki

	Title	Author
07-07	The Changing World Economy and Implications for Korea	Anne O. Krueger
07-08	The Longest Recovery of the Japanese Economy: Prospects and Challenges	Yukiko Fukagawa
07-09	Digital Networked Economy and Global Corporate Strategy	Ben Verwaayen
07-10	Moving Forward on the KORUS FTA: Now for the Hard Time	Jeffrey Schott
07-11	The Korean Economy and the FTA with the United States	Barry Eichengreen
07-12	- The Outlook for East Asian Economic Integration: Coping with American Protectionism, Chinese Power, and Japanese Recovery - Economic Outlook for Korea and the Region	- David Hale - Jerald Schiff
07-13	- Why the US Will Continue to Lead the 21st Century? - The Outlook of the Indian Economy from Business Perspective: Implications for Korean Business	- Guy Sorman - Tarun Das

2008

	Title	Author
08-01	Successes of Globalization: the Case of Korea	Anne O. Krueger
08-02	The US "Risk" to Asia and Global Expansion	Allen Sinai
08-03	Europe's Slow Growth: A Warning for Korea	Guy Sorman
08-04	Global Challenges that Will Confront the Next US President	James A. Baker III
08-05	Current Status and Prospects of the Japanese Capital Markets	Atsushi Saito
08-06	Economic and Political Outlook for America and their Implications to the World	Phil Gramm
08-07	The Outlook of the Regional and Global Economic and Financial Situation: Perspectives on International Banking	Charles Dallara
08-08	Can South Korea Still Compete?	Guy Sorman
08-09	- Sovereign Wealth Funds: Perceptions and Realities - Global Financial Markets under Stress	- Robert C. Pozen - Jeffrey R. Shafer

2009

	Title	Author
09-01	Global and Regional Economic Developments and Prospects, and the Implications for Korea	Subir Lall
09-02	Competing in an Era of Turbulence and Transition	Deborah Wince-Smith
09-03	US and Global Economic and Financial Crisis: Prospects, Policies, and Perspectives	Allen Sinai
09-04	US Trade Policy in the Obama Era	Jeffrey Schott
09-05	Beyond Keynesianism	Justin Yifu Lin
09-06	- Current Crisis and the Impact on Developing Countries - Lessons from the Current Economic Crisis	- Danny Leipziger - Anne O. Krueger
09-07	- Obama, Can It Work? - The US-Korea Economic Partnership: Working Together in a Time of Global Crisis	- Guy Sorman - Jeffrey Schott

2010

	Title	Author
10-01	The EU in Transition in the New Global Paradigm: Opportunities for Korea	Jean-Pierre Lehmann
10-02	Aftermath of the 'Crises': US and Global Prospects, Legacies, and Policies	Allen Sinai
10-03	The Global Economy: Where Do We Stand?	Anne O. Krueger
10-04	- Japan and Korea in Globalization and its Backlash: Challenges and Prospects - An Overview of China: Economic Prospects and Challenges	- Yukiko Fukagawa - Danny Leipziger
10-05	- Emerging Markets and New Frontiers - Asia in the Global Economy	- Mark Mobius - Dominique Strauss-Kahn
10-06	Rebalancing the World Economy	Paul A. Volcker

2011

	Title	Author
11-01	After the Crisis: What Next in 2011 and 2012?	Allen Sinai
11-02	Safety and Economics of Nuclear Power	SoonHeung Chang
11-03	A Special Lecture on the Rebalancing of the Chinese Economy	Yu Yongding

	Title	Author
11-04	Reshaping the Global Financial Landscape: An Asian Perspective	Institute for Global Economics
11-05	- Economic Outlook and Future Challenges in Developing Asia - Europe's Financial Woes	- Haruhiko Kuroda - Richard N. Cooper
11-06	- Can the G20 Save Globalization and Multilateralism? - Markets, Economic Changes, and Political Stability in North Korea	- Danny Leipziger - Marcus Noland

2012

	Title	Author
12-01	US and Global Economy and Financial Markets in Turmoil: What Lies Ahead?	Allen Sinai
12-02	- Advancement and Education of Science and Technology University and Economic Growth - Prospects of the Eurozone Crisis and its Implications for the Global Economy	- Nam Pyo Suh - Hans Martens
12-03	- The US Elections in 2012 and the Future of US Asia-Pacific Policy - Current Economic Affairs and the Financial Market - An Optimist View on the Global Economy	- Charles Morrison - Charles Dallara - Guy Sorman
12-04	- FTAs, Asia-Pacific Integration and Korea - The Eurozone Crisis: Update and Outlook	- Peter A. Petri - Nicolas Véron
12-05	- China's New Leadership and Economic Policy Challenges - Can the WTO Be Resuscitated? Implications for Korea and the Asia Pacific	- Andrew Sheng - Jean-Pierre Lehmann

2013

	Title	Author
13-01	After the Crisis: What Next in 2011 and 2012?	Allen Sinai
13-02	The Eurozone Crisis and its Impact on the Global Economy	Guntram B. Wolff
13-03	- The European Sovereign Debt Crisis: Challenges and How to Solve Them - The Global Outlook: Grounds for Optimism, but Risks Remain Relevant	- Andreas Dombret - John Lipsky
13-04	- The State and Outlook of the US and Chinese Economy - Japan's Abenomics and Foreign Policy	- David Hale - Hugh Patrick/ Gerald Curtis

	Title	Author
13-05	- The Creative Economy and Culture in Korea - Abenomics, Future of the Japanese Economy and the TPP	- Guy Sorman - Yukiko Fukagawa/ Jeffrey Schott
13-06	- Unified Germany in Europe: An Economic Perspective - Chinese Economic Policymaking: A Foreigners' Perspective	- Karl-Heinz Paqué - Bob Davis
13-07	- The Outlook for Japan under Abenomics and Abenationalism - After the Pax Americana (Korea-China-Japan Political and Economic Relation: Whither to?)	- David Asher - David Filling

2014

	Title	Author
14-01	U.S. and Global Economics-Poised for Better Times	Allen Sinai
14-02	- Abe in the Driver's Seat: Where is the Road Leading? - The Secret of Germany's Performance: The Mittelstand Economy	- Gerald Curtis - Peter Friedrich
14-03	- The Eurozone Economy: Out of the Doldrums? - The Globla Economy 2014	- Karl-Heinz Paqué - Martin Feldstein
14-04	Philanthropy and Welfare	Guy Sorman
14-05	- Global Trade Environment and the Future of the World Economy - From BRICs to America	- Roberto Azevêdo - Sung Won Sohn
14-06	- Risks and Opportunities in the Global Economic Recovery - Abe's Labor Reform and Innovative Strategies	- Charles Dallara - Yukiko Fukagawa
14-07	- China's Economy and Anti-Corruption Drive	- Bob Davis
	- US Fed's QE Ending & Asian Financial Markets	- Anoop Singh
	- China's New Economic Strategies and the Korea-China FTA	- Zhang Yunling

2015

	Title	Author
15-01	- Will the Global Economy Normalize in 2015?	- Allen Sinai
15-02	- The EU Economy in 2015: Will It Take Off? - U.S.-Korea Economic Relations: Partnership for Shared Economic Prosperity - The Hartz Labor Reforms of Germany and the Implications for Korea	- Jeroen Dijsselbloem - Mark W. Lippert - Peter Hartz
15-03	- What Makes China Grow? - What can Korea Learn from Europe's Slow Growth?	- Lawrence Lau - Guy Sorman

	Title	Author
15-04	- Global Energy and Environmental Issues and Switzerland - The Emerging New Asian Economic Disorder	- H.E. Doris Leuthard - David L. Asher
15-05	- The Chinese Economy: Transition towards the New Normal - Germany's Industry 4.0: Harnessing the Potential of Digitization	- Huang Yiping - Matthias Machnig
15-06	- Four Global Forces Changing the World - Turbulence in Emerging Markets and Impact on Korea	- Dominic Barton - Sung-won Sohn
15-07	- Observations on the Korean Economy and North Korea's Economic Potential - Perspectives on China's Economy and Economic Reform	- Thomas Byrne - Huang Haizhou

2016

	Title	Author
16-01	- The U.S. and Global Prospects and Markets in 2016: A Look Ahead	- Allen Sinai
16-02	- The Key Themes and Risks of the Global Economy in 2016 - The U.S. in the Global Economy	- Hung Tran - Anne Krueger
16-03	- The Prospects and Impact of the U.S. Election and Economy - The US and Northeast Asia in a Turbulent Time	- Martin Feldstein - Gerald Curtis
16-04	- The U.S. Presidential Election and Its Economic and Security Implications - The World Economy at a Time of Monetary Experimentation and Political Fracture - Allies in Business: The Future of the U.S.-ROK Economic Relationship	- Marcus Noland & Sung-won Sohn - Charles Dallara - Mark Lippert

2017

	Title	Author
17-01	- Big Changes, Big Effects - U.S. and Global Economic and Financial Prospects 2017	- Allen Sinai
17-02	- The 2017 US and Global Macroeconomic Outlook - Automation, Jobs and the Future of Work in Korea	- Martin Feldstein - Jonathan Woetzel
17-03	- Trump's US, Japan's Economy and Korea - Between Brexit and Trump: Global Challenges for the European Union	- Gerald Curtis & Hugh Paztrick - Thomas Wieser
17-04	- The Future of Work: Is This Time Different?	- Carl Benedikt Frey

	Title	Author
17-05	- The Future of Growth - The Current State of US Economy and Trump Administration's Trade Policy with Special Reference to the KORUS FTA Revision	- Simon Baptist - Sung-won Sohn & Jeffrey Schott

2018

	Title	Author
18-01	- Dr. Martin Feldstein's Analysis of the US and Global Economy - U.S. and Global Prospects Looking Ahead	- Martin Feldstein - Allen Sinai
18-02	- US Protectionism, China's Political Shift and Their Implications - Japan's Labor Reform and Future Korea-Japan Cooperation	- Kenneth Courtis - Yukiko Fukagawa
18-03	- U.S. Economic and Trade Policy for Korea and Asia - How Europeans See China, Changing World Order and Its Implications for Korea	- Charles Freeman - Guy Sorman
18-04	- Asia's New Economic Landscape: India, Japan and China - Climate, Energy and Green Tech: Transforming Our Economies	- Eisuke Sakakibara - Karsten Sach

2019

	Title	Author
19-01	- Financial Innovation, FinTech and the Future of Finance - Setting up Canada's National Pension System for Success – CPPIB's Perspectives	- Robert Merton - Suyi Kim
19-02	- Why I Remain Optimistic about China: Why China's Worst Enemy in the Short-Term Will Prove its Best Friend in the Long-Term - The World in 2019: U.S., Global Economies, Policies and Markets – Can Expansion be sustained?	- Henny Sender - Allen Sinai
19-03	- A Brief Tour of Global Near-term Risks and Long-run Concerns about the International Financial Architecture - 5 Ways the Financial System Will Fail Next Time	-Carmen Reinhart -Michael Barr
19-04	- Beyond 1980's: The New Horizon of Japan-Korea Economic Relations - Reflections on the Japanese Economy and Abenomics	-Yukiko Fukagawa -Hugh Patrick
19-05	- Financial Innovation and Asset Management Strategies in the Age of Hyper-Low Interest Rates	- Robert Merton
19-06	- Artificial Intelligence (AI) and its Impact on the Future of Economy and Society - U.S.-China, Korea-Japan Trade Disputes and the Global Trading System	- Jerome Glenn - Jeffrey Schott

Proceedings and Reports

	Title	Author
94-01	The Global Economy and Korea	Il SaKong
94-02	The Political Economy of Korea-US Cooperation	Il SaKong/ C. Fred Bergsten
95-01	International Next Generation Leaders Forum [I]	Institute for Global Economics
95-02	International Next Generation Leaders Forum [II]	Institute for Global Economics
95-03	Korea-US Cooperation in the New World Order	Il SaKong/ C. Fred Bergsten
96-01	The Multilateral Trading and Financial System	Il SaKong
96-02	Korea-US Relations in the Globalization Era	Il SaKong/ C. Fred Bergsten
96-03	International Next Generation Leaders Forum [III]	Institute for Global Economics
96-04	Is the Korean Semiconductor Industry in a Trap and Can It Get Out?	Institute for Global Economics
97-01	Major Issues for the Global Trade and Financial System	Il SaKong
97-02	Financial Reform in Korea	Institute for Global Economics
98-01	International Next Generation Leaders Forum [IV]	Institute for Global Economics
98-02	Korean Unification and the Current Status and Challenges for Korea-US Relationship	Il SaKong
98-03	Policy Priorities for the Unified Korean Economy	Il SaKong/ KwangSeok Kim
98-04	The Fifty Years of the GATT/WTO: Past Performance and Future Challenges	Il SaKong/ KwangSeok Kim
99-01	Asian Financial Crisis: Causes and Policy Implications	Il SaKong/ Young Hun Koo
99-02	The Asian Financial Crisis and Korea-US Relations	Institute for Global Economics
99-03	For a Better Tomorrow: Asia-Europe Partnership in the 21st Century	ASEM Vision Group
00-01	Reforming the International Financial Architecture: Emerging Market perspectives	Il SaKong/ Yunjong Wang
00-02	Northeast Asia Forum 2000	Institute for Global Economics

	Title	Author
00-03	Proceedings of the Sixth Korea-US 21st Century Council Meeting	Institute for Global Economics
01-01	Building Constituencies for a Global Liberal Trade Agenda	Institute for Global Economics
01-02	Rebuilding the International Financial Architecture (EMEPG Seoul Report)	Emerging Markets Eminent Persons Group
03-01	The New World Order and Korea [I]	Institute for Global Economics
03-02	The New World Order and Korea [II]	Institute for Global Economics
03-03	The New World Order and Korea [III]	Institute for Global Economics
03-04	IGE's 10th Anniversary International Conference	Institute for Global Economics
04-01	How to Facilitate Business Start-ups	Institute for Global Economics
08-01	Globalization and Korean Financial Sector	Institute for Global Economics
09-01	Lessons from the Recent Global Financial Crisis: Its Implications for the World and Korea	Institute for Global Economics
10-01	G20 Reform Initiatives: Implications for the Future of Financial Regulation	Institute for Global Economics
10-02	G20 Seoul Summit and Development Agenda	Institute for Global Economics
12-01	New Global Financial Regulatory Regime in the Making: Impact on Asian Financial Markets and Institutions	Institute for Global Economics
12-02	Culture, Korean Economy and the Korean Wave	Institute for Global Economics
12-03	Asia in the New Global Financial Scene	Institute for Global Economics
13-01	Fostering Hidden Champions: Lessons from German Experiences	Institute for Global Economics
13-02	Unification and the Korean Economy	Institute for Global Economics
13-03	The 20-Year Report of Activities	Institute for Global Economics
14-01	Leadership & Policy Priorities	Institute for Global Economics

	Title	Author
15-01	Women and Growth Potential	Institute for Global Economics
17-01	The Fourth Industrial Revolution and the Future of the Korean Economy	Institute for Global Economics
19-01	The Future of Digital Finance and FinTech Industry: Towards Busan FinTech Hub	Kwang-woo Jun

IGE Brief+

2012

	Title	Author
12-01	Culture Industry, Service Trade and the Korean Economy	Chong-Hyun Nam
12-02	Korea-Japan Economic Integration: Trend and Prospect	Jongyun Lee
12-03	The Eurozone Crisis and Challenges for Korea	Jung-Taik Hyun
12-04	Korea's Presidential Election 2012: Why Is It More Critical This Time?	Il SaKong
12-05	Financial Consumer Protection and the Financial Ombudsman Service	JaeUng Lee
12-06	We Must Be Prepared for the Korean Unification	Il SaKong

2013

	Title	Author
13-01	New World Economic Order and Forward-looking Korea-Japan Relationship	Il SaKong
13-02	Financial Reform and China's Political Economy	Yoon-Je Cho

2014

	Title	Author
14-01	No Future for a Society that isn't Alarmed at Attacks against Police	Il SaKong
14-02	To Make the 3-Year Agenda for Economic Reform Successful	Il SaKong
14-03	Reinventing Korea for a Trustworthy Nation	Il SaKong
14-04	Reemergence of China: Challenges and Opportunities	Il SaKong

2016

	Title	Author
16-01	Korea in the Rapidly Changing World and Surroundings	Il SaKong

Global Economic Horizons

1994

	Title	Author
94-01	Challenges of a Nomadic World	Jacques Attali
94-02	Globalism vs. Regionalism	YoungSun Lee
94-03	Prospects for the Chinese Market	Wan-soon Kim
94-04	How to Prepare for the 21st Century	Paul Kennedy
94-05	Death of Money/Post Capitalist Society	GiTaek Hong/ HanGwang Joo
94-06	Asia-Pacific Economic Cooperation in the Post-UR Era	Yoo Jae Won
94-07	Environment and Trade	Seong-Lin Na/ SeungJin Kim
94-08	Structural Adjustment in Japan and the Korean Economy	JongYoon Lee
94-09	Changes in the Global Economic Environment and Options for Korea	Il SaKong
94-10	Market Opening and Management Policy in Korea	JongSeok Kim

1995

	Title	Author
95-01	Korea's Economy and its New Global Responsibilities	Il SaKong
95-02	Globalization and Competition Norm of the Enterprises	Wan-soon Kim
95-03	What is Globalization?	ByungJoo Kim
95-04	Korea and the US: The Year 2000 in the Global Economy	James Laney
95-05	Will the World Economy Collapse?	ChukKyo Kim
95-06	Possibility of Continuously Strong Yen and Korea's Countermeasures	Jin-Geun Park
95-07	Globalization and the Korean Economy: Boom or Bubble?	BonHo Koo
95-08	Preferential Trade Agreements and Policy Measures	Chong-Hyun Nam
95-09	Historical Consciousness and Korea-Japan Relations	WonTack Hong
95-10	Japan's Industrial Network Organizations and its Efficiency	JongYoon Lee
95-11	Dilemmas of International Competition	JaeUng Lee

	Title	Author
95-12	Overview of the Post-Liberation Korean Economy and Prospects for the Future	KwangSeok Kim

1996

	Title	Author
96-01	The Domestic Futures Market: Its Planning and Prospects	Sun Lee
96-02	Will the Era for Medium-sized Firms Be Opened?	Dong-Gil Yoo
96-03	On the Collective Bargaining System of Korea	MooGi Bae
96-04	Globalization and Transformation of Businesses	Cheong Ji
96-05	Liberalization of the Financial Markets in Korea	YoungCheol Park
96-06	Multilateralism vs. Regionalism: Can It Be Compatible?	SeWon Kim
96-07	Risks and Effectiveness of the Financial Derivatives	SangKee Min
96-08	Recent Economic Crisis and Policy Measures	KwangSeok Kim
96-09	Economic Development, Policy Reform and the Establishment of Competition Order	SeongSeob Lee
96-10	The Role of Government in Transition	ByeongJu Kim
96-11	New Agenda of the WTO	WanSoon Kim

1997

	Title	Author
97-01	How to Solve the Labor Law Revision?	SooGon Kim
97-02	Why a Low Economic Growth Rate is Desirable	ChukKyo Kim
97-03	Lessons from the Hanbo Crisis	JaeUng Lee
97-04	Economic Management in the Era of Globalization	DeokWoo Nam
97-05	A True Story of Company Growth: Lessons from the Hanbo Crisis	Cheong Ji
97-06	North Korea's Food Crisis and Collective Farming	PalYong Moon
97-07	Korea's Financial Sector Reform	KeSop Yun
97-08	An Aging Population and the Budget Crisis	Jong-Gi Park
97-09	Korea's Response Strategies Based on a General Model of Foreign Exchange Crisis	JinGeun Park
97-10	How to Open an Era of Ventures	Dong-Gil Yoo

1998

	Title	Author
98-01	Has Korea's Economic Miracle Ended?	Chong-Hyun Nam
98-02	The Impossibility of Overcoming a Crisis without a Grand Paradigm Shift	DaeHee Song
98-03	Corporate Restructuring and Desirable Relationships between Banks and Corporations	SangWoo Nam
98-04	A Search for New Corporate Governance and Roles of Outside Directors	Yeong-gi Lee
98-05	Suggestions for Breaking the Circle of High Investments and High Savings	YeongTak Lee

1999

	Title	Author
99-01	Prospects and Agenda for Pension Reform	Jong-Ki Park
99-02	The Subway Strike and Review of Issues Regarding Full Time Unionists	Soo-Gon Kim
99-03	Financial Restructuring and Financing for Small- and Medium-sized Firms	JunGyeong Park
99-04	Environmental Policy Agenda for the 21st Century	Jong-Ki Kim
99-05	How to Deal with Income Distribution Problems in Korea	KwangSeok Kim
99-06	Fallacy and Reality in Productive Social Welfare System	Kwang Choi
99-07	Toward Closer Economic Cooperation among Korea, China and Japan in the Age of Globalization	Il SaKong
99-08	WTO New Round - Recent Ministerial Meeting in Seattle and its Prospect	Tae-ho Bark

2000

	Title	Author
00-01	The Prospect and Policy Alternatives for the Korean Economy 2000	Joon-Kyung Kim
00-02	What Happened to the Debate on the Global Financial Architecture?	Il SaKong
00-03	The Recent Financial Crisis and Korea's Economic Future	Il SaKong
00-04	Revisit of High Cost with Low Efficiency	JongYun Lee
00-05	Is Asia's Recovery Sustainable?	Il SaKong

	Title	Author
00-06	The International Economic Environment and Korean Economic Development	Yoon-Je Cho
00-07	The Role of International Investors in the Evolution of Corporate Governance in Korea	JaeUng Lee
00-08	US Restructuring Experience and Lessons	YeongSe Lee

2001

	Title	Author
01-01	A Perspective of Korean Industries and Strategies for Industrial Development	DoHoon Kim
01-02	Reconsidering Working Five Days a Week	Young-bum Park

Research Reports (Global Economy Series)

1994

	Title	Author
94-01	The Task of Asia-Pacific Economic Cooperation in the Post-UR Era and Policy Options for Korea	JaeWon Yoo
94-02	Current Discussions on Environment - Trade Relations and its Implications for Korean Trade	SeungJin Kim/ SeongRin Na
94-03	Japan's Structural Adjustments to a Strong Yen and Strategies for the Korean Economy	JongYun Lee
94-04	Market Opening and Management Policy in Korea	JongSeok Kim

1995

	Title	Author
95-01	Foreign Direct Investment in Korea: Its Current Status and Policy Recommendations	HanGwang Joo/ SeungJin Kim
95-02	Receptivity of Business Process Re-engineering in Korean and Japanese Firms	JaeGyu Lee
95-03	The World Trade Organization Regime and Korea's Strategy	JiHong Kim

1996

	Title	Author
96-01	The Domestic Futures Market: Its Planning and Prospects	Sun Lee
96-02	Japan's Industrial Network Organization and its Efficiency: A Case Study of the Automobile Industry	JongYun Lee

1997

	Title	Author
97-01	Romania's Economic Situation and Major Reform Issues	GwangSeok Kim/ ByeongJi Kim/ IlDong Koh

1998

	Title	Author
98-01	Sources of Korea's Economic Growth and Future Growth Potentials	KwangSeok Kim
98-02	Trade Patterns between Korea and ASEAN Countries: Their Changes and Korea's Response	SeungJin Kim
98-03	The Global Trading System: Challenges Ahead	WanSoon Kim/ NakGyun Choi
98-04	International Trends in the Information Society and Korea's Strategy	JongGuk Park

2000

	Title	Author
00-01	Financial Crisis and Industry Policy in Korea	YeongSe Lee / YongSeung Jeong

2001

	Title	Author
01-01	Korea's Industrial and Trade Policies: Their Evolution from 1961 to 1999	KwangSeok Kim
01-02	Technology Transfer and the Role of Information in Korea	YeongSe Lee

Special Lecture Series

1993

No.	Date	Title	Speaker
93-01	Feb 11	Clintonomics and the New World Order: Implications for Korea-US Relations	C. Fred Bergsten
93-02	Mar 18	The Uruguay Round, NAFTA and US-Korea Economic Relations	Jeffrey Schott
93-03	Apr 9	The Economy and Financial Markets: Outlook and Issues	Allen Sinai
93-04	Jun 22	Economic Outlook for the Pacific and Implications for Korea	Lawrence Krauss
93-05	Nov 4	Challenges of a Nomadic World	Jacques Attali

1994

No.	Date	Title	Speaker
94-01	Jan 5	Korea in the World: Today and Tomorrow	Paul Kennedy
94-02	Mar 22	US-Japan Technological Competition and Implications for Korea	Ronald A. Morse
94-03	Mar 25	The Problems of the Japanese Economy and their Implications for Korea	Toyoo Gyohten
94-04	Apr 18	Changing US and World Economies and their Market Prospects	Allen Sinai
94-05	Jun 28	Prospects for East European Economy and Implications for Korea	Ronald Freeman
94-06	Sep 6	Prospects for New World Monetary System and Implications for Korea	John Williamson
94-07	Oct 18	Prospects for New Trade Order and Implications for Korea	Arthur Dunkel
94-08	Dec 15	Financial Reform for the New Economy: Evaluations and Prospects	Jaeyoon Park

1995

No.	Date	Title	Speaker
95-01	Jan 26	Strategies for Globalization and Future Economic Policy	JaeHyong Hong
95-02	Jan 27	Mexican Peso Crisis and its Implications for the Global Financial Market	Charles Dallara

No.	Date	Title	Speaker
95-03	Mar 6	The World Economic Trend and US Economic Outlook	Allen Sinai
95-04	Mar 29	Korea and US: The Year 2000 in the Global Economy	James Laney
95-05	Apr 11	New Games, New Rules, and New Strategies	Lester Thurow
95-06	Apr 21	The United States and North Korea Future Prospects	Robert Scalapino
95-07	May 18	US Foreign Policy toward East Asia and the Korean Peninsula	James A. Baker III
95-08	Jun 14	New World Trade Regime in the Post-UR Era and its Implications for Korea	Anne O. Krueger
95-09	Jun 20	International Financial System after Mexico and Recent Currency Crisis	Stanley Fischer
95-10	Jul 19	The World Trade Organization - New Challenges	Jagdish Bhagwati
95-11	Sep 1	Prospects for Northeast Asian Development and the Role of Korea	Hisao Kanamori
95-12	Oct 17	Russian Intelligence System: Past Performance and Future Prospects	Vadim Kirpitchenko
95-13	Oct 19	Trends of the International Financial Market and Prospects of Global Economy	Allen Sinai
95-14	Nov 7	Current US Political Trends and their Implications for US-Korea Relations	Thomas Foley
95-15	Nov 13	APEC and the World Multilateral Trading System	C. Fred Bergsten
95-16	Nov 28	International Monetary Regime - Current Status and Future Prospects	Toyoo Gyohten
95-17	Dec 6	WTO and the World Trading System - Where Do We Go from Here?	Anne O. Krueger

1996

No.	Date	Title	Speaker
96-01	Jan 25	Challenges for the Global Trading System	Robert Lawrence
96-02	Feb 1	Trade Polices of the New Economy	Jaeyoon Park
96-03	Feb 26	Technology Issues in the International Trading System	Sylvia Ostry
96-04	Mar 19	Information Era: Korea's Strategies	Sukchae Lee

No.	Date	Title	Speaker
96-05	Apr 9	Future European Model: Economic Internationalization and Culture Decentralization	Jørgen Ørstrøm Møller
96-06	Apr 23	Evolving Role of the OECD in the Global Economy	Donald Johnston
96-07	May 7	New Issues for the Multilateral Trading System: Singapore and Beyond	Chulsu Kim
96-08	May 17	Financial Globalization and World Economy: Implications for Korea	Paul A. Volker
96-09	May 21	Cooperation or Conflict? - A European Perspective on East Asia's Place in the Global Economy	Martin Wolf
96-10	May 23	East Asia in Overdrive: Multinationals and East Asian Integrations	Wendy Dobson
96-11	May 28	Japan's Banking Difficulties: Causes and Implications	Hugh Patrick
96-12	Jun 29	The Political Context and Consequences of East Asian Economic Growth	Francis Fukuyama
96-13	Jul 9	President Clinton's First Term and Prospects for a Second: Implications for Korea	Robert Warne
96-14	Sep 17	Global Free Trade: A Vision for the Early 21st Century	C. Fred Bergsten
96-15	Oct 22	Korea's New Global Responsibilities	A. W. Clausen
96-16	Nov 26	The Free Trade Area of Clinton's Second Term: Implications for APEC and Korea	Richard Feinberg

1997

No.	Date	Title	Speaker
97-01	Feb 25	Economic management in the Era of Globalization	Duckwoo Nam
97-02	Mar 18	German Unification: Economic Consequences and Policy Lessons	Juergen B. Donges
97-03	May 27	American Security Policy in the Asia Pacific- Three Crisis and How We Dealt With Them	William Perry
97-04	Jun 10	Global Cooperations and National Government: Why We Need Multilateral Agreement on Investment	Edward Graham
97-05	Jul 8	Public Sector Reform in New Zealand and its Relevance to Korea	Donald Hunn

No.	Date	Title	Speaker
97-06	Sep 18	Korean-American Relations: The Search for Stability at a Time of Change	W. Anthony Lake
97-07	Oct 21	Korea: From Vortex to Hub of Northeast Asia	Donald P. Gregg
97-08	Dec 9	The Japanese Economic Slump and Currency Crises in Other East Asian Economies	Ronald McKinnon

1998

No.	Date	Title	Speaker
98-01	Jan 14	Globalization and versus Tribalization: The Dilemma at the End of the 20th Century	Guy Sorman
98-02	Feb 3	Asian Currency Turmoil and Japan's Role	Takatoshi Kato
98-03	Feb 5	The Asian Financial Crisis and Challenges Facing Korea: From An American Perspective	Charles Dallara
98-04	Apr 28	The Significance of the European Economic Monetary Union: in Europe and Beyond	Tue Rohsted
98-05	Jun 23	Asian Currency Crisis: What Has Happened?	Anne O. Krueger
98-06	Sep 17	How to Reform Public Sector Management	Nyum Jin
98-07	Dec 4	Economic Outlook for 1999: Asia and Korea	Hubert Neiss
98-08	Dec 11	North Korea in Global Perspective	Marcus Noland

1999

No.	Date	Title	Speaker
99-01	Feb 11	Korea in the World Economy: An OECD Appreciation of its Newest Member	Donald Johnston
99-02	Mar 5	Prospects for US Stock Exchanges and US Economy	Richard A. Grasso
99-03	Apr 6	The International Financial Market and the US Dollar/Yen Exchange Rate: An Overview and Prospects for the Future	Kenneth S. Courtis
99-04	May 19	Reflections on Contrasting Present-day US and Japanese Economic Performances	Hugh Patrick
99-05	Jul 22	Challenge for the World Economy: Where Do the Risks Lie?	Rudiger Dornbusch

No.	Date	Title	Speaker
99-06	Oct 5	How Should Korea Cope With Financial Globalization	James P. Rooney
99-07	Dec 2	Global Financial Market: Current Status and Prospects	Robert Hormats
99-08	Dec 14	North Korea-US Relationship: Its Current Condition and Future Prospects	Stephen W. Bosworth

2000

No.	Date	Title	Speaker
00-01	Jan 19	The Outlook for Asia and Other Emerging Markets in 2000	Charles Dallara
00-02	Feb 15	Global New Economy: Challenges and Opportunities for Korea	Soogil Young
00-03	Feb 29	Asia Grows, and Japan Slows- Prospect for the World Economy and Markets	Kenneth S. Courtis
00-04	Mar 28	The Future of International Financial System and its Implications for Korea	Morris Goldstein
00-05	Apr 26	Policies toward Continued Corporate and Financial Reform	Youngkeun Lee
00-06	May 26	Prospects for Millenium Round Trade Negotiations and Korea-US Free Trade Agreement	Jeffrey Schott
00-07	Jun 23	Prospects for Multilateral Economic Institutions	Anne O. Krueger
00-08	Jul 13	Avoiding the Apocalypse: The Future of the Two Koreas	Marcus Noland
00-09	Sep 14	Attracting FDI in the Knowledge Era	Andrew Fraser
00-10	Nov 10	The Economic and Foreign Policies of the New US Administration and Congress	C. Fred Bergsten

2001

No.	Date	Title	Speaker
01-01	Feb 6	The US Economy on the Brink? Japan on the Edge? Implications for Asian and the World Economy	Kenneth S. Courtis
01-02	Feb 27	Economic Policy of the Bush Administration toward Korea	Marcus Noland
01-03	Apr 26	Jeffrey Jones' Evaluation of Korean Business and Economy: Overcoming Three 'C's	Jeffrey D. Jones

No.	Date	Title	Speaker
01-04	Jun 5	High Tech, The Consequences of our Relationship with Technology on our Lives and Businesses	John Naisbitt
01-05	Jul 9	Korea and the IMF	Stanley Fischer
01-06	Jul 19	Outlook on Korea Over the Next Ten Years	Dominic Barton
01-07	Sep 4	The World Dollar Standard and the East Asian Exchange Rate Dilemma	Roland McKinnon
01-08	Oct 9	Europe's Role in Global Governance and Challenges to East Asia/Korea	Pierre Jacquet
01-09	Nov 6	Globalization and Dangers in the World Economy	Martin Wolf
01-10	Nov 16	Preventing Financial Crises: The Chilean Perspective	Carlos Massad
01-11	Nov 20	The New US-Japan Economic Relationship and Implications for Korea	Marcus Noland

2002

No.	Date	Title	Speaker
02-01	Jan 9	Globalization: A Force for Good	Patricia Hewitt
02-02	Jan 16	The World After 9/11: A Clash of Civilizations?	Francis Fukuyama
02-03	Feb 22	Hanging Together: On Monetary and Financial Cooperation in Asia	Barry Eichengreen
02-04	Apr 16	US and Global Recovery: For Real? Prospects and Risks	Allen Sinai
02-05	May 7	The Global Economy Rebounds - But How Fast and For How Long? Issues and Implications for Korea	Kenneth S. Courtis
02-06	Jun 14	The US Economy and the Future of the Dollar	Marcus Noland
02-07	Jul 10	The Doha Round: Objectives, Problems and Prospects	Jagdish Bhagwati
02-08	Sep 24	The Outlook for Korea and the Global Economy 2002-2003	Paul F. Gruenwald
02-09	Oct 11	The Outlook for US Economy, the Dollar and US Trade Policy	C. Fred Bergsten
02-10	Oct 22	9/11 and the US Approach to the Korean Peninsula	Thomas C. Hubbard
02-11	Oct 24	The US and World Economy: Current Status and Prospects	John B. Taylor

No.	Date	Title	Speaker
02-12	Dec 3	New Challenges and Opportunities for the Global Telecommunications and Information Industries	Peter F. Cowhey

2003

No.	Date	Title	Speaker
03-01	Apr 8	The US and World Economy: After the Iraq War	Allen Sinai
03-02	May 30	2003 Global Economy and Key Economic Issues: From the OECD's Perspectives	Donald Johnston
03-03	Jun 10	The New Role of the US in the Asia-Pacific	Charles Morrison
03-04	Jul 4	Global Economic Outlook and the Impact of President Bush's Economic Stimulus Package	Phil Gramm
03-05	Oct 28	The Global Exchange Rate Regime and Implications for East Asian Currencies	John Williamson
03-06	Nov 4	Europe and Germany in Transition, Where Will the Economies Go?	Hans Tietmeyer
03-07	Nov 21	Regional Financial Cooperation in East Asia	Eisuke Sakakibara

2004

No.	Date	Title	Speaker
04-01	Feb 3	An Outlook for the US and World Economy in 2004	Allen Sinai
04-02	Apr 7	Korea After Kim Jong-il	Marcus Noland
04-03	Apr 21	A Foreign Businessman's Observations on Korean Economy and Other Things	William C. Oberlin
04-04	Jun 1	- The US Election, US-Japan Relations, and Implications for Korea - US Economic Performance, Japanese Economic Performance, and Implications for Korea	- Gerald Curtis - Hugh Patrick
04-05	Jul 13	China's Economic Rise and New Regional Growth Paradigm	Zhang Yunling
04-06	Oct 14	The Case for a Common Currency in Asia	Robert Mundell
04-07	Nov 2	Impact of the Presidential Election on US Trade Policy	Peter F. Cowhey
04-08	Dec 7	Asia in Transition and Implication for Korea	Dominic Barton

2005

No.	Date	Title	Speaker
05-01	Jan 18	Post-Election US and Global Economies and Markets Prospects, Risks, and Issues	Allen Sinai
05-02	Mar 2	The Korean Economy: A Critical Assessment from the Japanese Perspective	Yukiko Fukagawa
05-03	Apr 12	A Rating Agency Perspective on Korea	Thomas Byrne
05-04	May 10	The Impact of China and India on the World Economy	Wendy Dobson
05-05	May 31	Visions of East Asian and Asian-Pacific Integration: Competing or Complementary	Robert Scollay
05-06	Jun 30	Mutual Independence: Asia and the International Economy	Anne O. Krueger
05-07	Sep 1	The Blind Man and the Elephant: Competing Perspectives on Global Imbalances	Barry Eichengreen
05-08	Oct 13	Measuring American Power in Today's Complex World	Paul Kennedy
05-09	Oct 28	China "Rising": What Lessons for Today from the Past?	Bernard Gordon
05-10	Nov 15	Oil Prices, Ben Bernanke, Inflation, and the Fourth Energy Recession	Philip K. Verleger

2006

No.	Date	Title	Speaker
06-01	Jan 23	US Global Economy and Financial Market Prospects: Picking up Steam	Allen Sinai
06-02	Feb 14	Korea-US FTA: A Path to Sustainable Growth	Alexander Vershbow
06-03	Mar 28	Japan's Economic Recovery: Policy Implication for Korea	Yukiko Fukagawa
06-04	Apr 18	The Global Scramble for IT Leadership: Winners and Losers	George Scalise
06-05	May 10	Korea's Growing Stature in the Global Economy	Charles Dallara
06-06	Jun 20	Japan's Foreign Policy for Economy and Japan-Korea FTA	Oshima Shotaro
06-07	Jun 30	Whither China?	Richard N. Cooper
06-08	Jul 20	M&A in the 21st Century and its Implications	Rpbert F. Bruner

No.	Date	Title	Speaker
06-09	Sep 1	Korea and the US - Forging a Partnership for the Future: A View from Washington	Edwin J. Feulner
06-10	Sep 12	Asian Economic Integration and Common Asian Currency	Eisuke Sakakibara
06-11	Sep 15	Germany: Understanding the Economic Underperformance since Reunification	Juergen B. Donges
06-12	Sep 21	Changing Economic Environment and their Implications for Korea	Angel Gurría
06-13	Oct 12	The Feasibility of Establishing an East Asian FTA: A Chinese Perspective	Zhang Yunling
06-14	Nov 9	The Global Oil and Gas Market: Paradigm Shift and Implications for Korea	Fereidun Fesharaki
06-15	Nov 29	The Changing World Economy and its Implications for Korea	Anne O. Krueger

2007

No.	Date	Title	Speaker
07-01	Jan 9	Seismic Shifts, the World Economy, and Financial Markets in 2007	Allen Sinai
07-02	Feb 13	The Longest Recovery of the Japanese Economy: Prospects and Challenges	Yukiko Fukagawa
07-03	Mar 9	Digital Networked Economy and Global Corporate Strategy	Ben Verwaayen
07-04	May 3	The Outlook for East Asian Economic Integration: Coping with American Protectionism, Chinese Power, and Japanese Recovery	David Hale
07-05	May 8	Key Trend in the 2008 US Presidential Campaign	Stephen J. Yates
07-06	May 11	Strengthening Korea's Position in the Global Economy	Charles Dallara
07-07	Jun 21	Moving Forward the KORUS FTA: Now for the Hard Time	Jeffrey Schott
07-08	Aug 24	The Korea Economy and the FTA with the United States	Barry Eichengreen
07-09	Oct 4	Why the US Will Continue to Lead the 21st Century?	Guy Sorman
07-10	Oct 19	The Outlook of the Indian Economy from Business Perspective: Implications for Korean Business	Tarun Das

No.	Date	Title	Speaker
07-11	Oct 25	Globalization, Diversity and Recruitment of Business Talents	Ben Verwaayen
07-12	Nov 8	Economic Outlook for Korea and the Region	Jerald Schiff
07-13	Dec 14	Successes of Globalization: the Case of Korea	Anne O. Krueger

2008

No.	Date	Title	Speaker
08-01	Jan 15	The US "Risk" to Asia and the Global Expansion	Allen Sinai
08-02	Mar 25	Sovereign Wealth Funds: Perceptions and Realities	Robert C. Pozen
08-03	May 14	Europe's Slow Growth: A Warning for Korea	Guy Sorman
08-04	May 30	Global Challenges that Will Confront the Next US President	James A. Baker III
08-05	Jun 10	Current Status and Prospects of the Japanese Capital Market	Atsushi Saito
08-06	Jun 18	Economic and Political Outlook for America and their Implications to the World	Phil Gramm
08-07	Sep 17	The Outlook of the Regional and Global Economic and Financial Situation: Perspectives on International Banking	Charles Dallara
08-08	Sep 23	Can South Korea Still Compete?	Guy Sorman
08-09	Oct 17	Global Financial Markets under Stress	Jeffrey Shafer
08-10	Nov 4	Current Global Financial Crisis, the Dollar, and the Price of Oil	Martin Feldstein
08-11	Dec 9	Global and Regional Economic Development and Prospects, and the Implications for Korea	Subir Lall

2009

No.	Date	Title	Speaker
09-01	Jan 13	Competing in an Era of Turbulence and Transition	Deborah Wince-Smith
09-02	Feb 3	US and Global Economic and Financial Crisis: Prospects, Policies, and Perspectives	Allen Sinai

No.	Date	Title	Speaker
09-03	Feb 24	Current Crisis and the Impact on Developing Countries	Danny Leipziger
09-04	Feb 25	US Trade Policy in the Obama Era	Jeffrey Schott
09-05	Mar 19	Obama, Can It Work?	Guy Sorman
09-06	Apr 15	Lessons from the Current Economic Crisis	Anne O. Krueger
09-07	Jun 23	Beyond Keynesianism	Justin Yifu Lin
09-08	Jul 21	The US-Korea Economic Partnership: Working Together in a Time of Global Crisis	Jeffrey Schott
09-09	Aug 20	Prospects for Investment after the Current Economic Crisis: The Role of IFC and Developing Countries	Lars H. Thunell
09-10	Oct 15	Is a Double-Dip a Realistic Possibility?	SungWon Sohn
09-11	Dec 8	The EU in Transition in the New Global Paradigm: Opportunities for Korea?	Jean-Pierre Lehmann

2010

No.	Date	Title	Speaker
10-01	Jan 21	Aftermath of the 'Crisis': US and Global Prospects, Legacies, and Policies	Allen Sinai
10-02	Apr 8	Japan and Korea in Globalization and its Backlash: Challenges and Prospects	Yukiko Fukagawa
10-03	Apr 22	Emerging Markets and New Frontiers	Mark Mobius
10-04	May 18	An Overview of China: Economic Prospects and Challenges	Danny Leipziger
10-05	Jul 13	Asia in the Global Economy	Dominique Strauss-Kahn
10-06	Aug 31	The Global Economy: Where Do We Stand?	Anne O. Krueger
10-07	Oct 15	How Close Are We to a Double-Dip and Deflation?	SungWon Sohn
10-08	Nov 5	Rebalancing the World Economy	Paul A. Volcker

2011

No.	Date	Title	Speaker
11-01	Jan 20	After the Crisis: What Next in 2011 and 2012?	Allen Sinai

No.	Date	Title	Speaker
11-02	Feb 24	Economic Outlook and Future Challenges in Developing Asia	Haruhiko Kuroda
11-03	Mar 23	Europe's Financial Woes	Richard N. Cooper
11-04	Apr 28	Safety and Economics of Nuclear Power	SoonHeung Chang
11-05	May 24	Can the G20 Save Globalization and Multilateralism?	Danny Leipziger
11-06	Jun 29	Markets, Economic Changes, and Political Stability in North Korea	Marcus Noland
11-07	Aug 30	A Special Lecture on the Rebalancing of the Chinese Economy	Yu Yongding
11-08	Dec 31	Global Economic Turbulence and Investment Implications	SungWon Sohn

2012

No.	Date	Title	Speaker
12-01	Jan 19	US and Global Economy and Markets Turmoil: What Lies Ahead?	Allen Sinai
12-02	Mar 13	The US Elections in 2012 and the Future of US Asia-Pacific Policy	Charles Morrison
12-03	Jun 22	Advancement and Education of Science and Technology University and Economic Growth	NamPyo Suh
12-04	Jul 17	Prospects of the Eurozone Crisis and its Implications for the Global Economy	Hans Martens
12-05	Sep 14	Current Economic Affairs and the Financial Market	Charles Dallara
12-06	Sep 18	An Optimist View on the Global Economy	Guy Sorman
12-07	Oct 11	FTAs, Asia-Pacific Integration and Korea	Peter A. Petri
12-08	Oct 29	The Eurozone Crisis: Update and Outlook	Nicolas Veron
12-09	Nov 21	China's New Leadership and Economic Policy Challenges	Andrew Sheng
12-10	Dec 7	Can the WTO Be Resuscitated? Implications for Korea and the Asia Pacific	Jean-Pierre Lehmann

2013

No.	Date	Title	Speaker
13-01	Jan 10	The US and Global Economies after the US Election and in the New Year	Allen Sinai

No.	Date	Title	Speaker
13-02	Jan 17	The Eurozone Crisis and its Impact on the Global Economy	Guntram B. Wolff
13-03	Feb 8	The European Sovereign Debt Crisis: Challenges and How to Solve Them	Andreas Dombret
13-04	Mar 22	The Global Outlook: Grounds for Optimism, but Risks Remain Relevant	John Lipsky
13-05	Apr 3	The State and Outlook of the US and Chinese Economy	David Hale
13-06	Apr 9	Japan's Abenomics and Foreign Policy	Hugh Patrick/ Gerald Curtis
13-07	Apr 30	The Creative Economy and Culture in Korea	Guy Sorman
13-08	May 21	The Japanese Economy and Trans-Pacific Partnership (TPP)	Yukiko Fukagawa/ Jeffrey Schott
13-09	Jun 27	Unified Germany in Europe: An Economic Perspective	Karl-Heinz Paqué
13-10	Jul 19	Chinese Economic Policymaking: A Foreigner's Perspective	Bob Davis
13-11	Sep 27	Japanese Politics and Abenomics Implications for Korea and the World	David Asher
13-12	Nov 15	Korea-China-Japan Economic and Political Relations: Wither to?	David Philling

2014

No.	Date	Title	Speaker
14-01	Jan 7	U.S. and Global Economies - Poised for Better Times?	Allen Sinai
14-02	Jan 14	Swiss Made	R. James Breiding
14-03	Feb 20	Abe in the Driver's Seat: Where is the Road Leading?	Gerald Curtis
14-04	Feb 26	The Secret of Germany's Performance: The Mittlestand Economy	Peter Friedrich
14-05	Mar 5	The Eurozone Economy: Out of Doldrums?	Karl-Heinz Paqué
14-06	Mar 17	The Global Economy 2014	Martin Feldstein
14-07	Apr 3	Philanthropy and Welfare	Guy Sorman
14-08	May 16	Global Trade Environment and the Future of the World Economy	Roberto Azevedo
14-09	May 23	From BRICs to America	SungWon Sohn

No.	Date	Title	Speaker
14-10	Jul 24	Risks and Opportunities in the Global Economic Recovery	Charles Dallara
14-11	Sep 12	Abe's Labor Reform and Innovative Strategies	Yukiko Fukagawa
14-12	Sep 26	a's Economy and Anti-Corruption Drive	Bob Davis
14-13	Oct 17	US Fed's QE Ending & Asian Financial Markets	Anoop Singh
14-14	Nov 14	China's New Economic Strategy and the Korea-China FTA	Zhang Yunlingng

2015

No.	Date	Title	Speaker
15-01	Jan 15	The EU Economy in 2015: Will It Take Off?	Jeroen Dijsselbloem
15-02	Jan 20	Will the Global Economy Normalize in 2015?	Allen Sinai
15-03	Apr 24	What Makes China Grow?	Lawrence Lau
15-04	Apr 28	U.S.-Korea Economic Relations: Partnership for Shared Economic Prosperity	Mark W. Lippert
15-05	May 5	The Hartz Labor Reforms of Germany and the Implications for Korea	Peter Hartz
15-06	Jun 2	What can Korea Learn from Europe's Slow Growth?	Guy Sorman
15-07	Jul 9	Global Energy and Environmental Issues and Switzerland	Doris Leuthard
15-08	Sep 11	The Emerging New Asian Economic Disorder	David L. Asher
15-09	Sep 21	The Chinese Economy: Transition towards the New Normal	Huang Yiping
15-10	Oct 13	Germany's Industry 4.0: Harnessing the Potential of Digitization	Matthias Machnig
15-11	Oct 29	Four Global Forces Changing the World	Dominic Barton
15-12	Nov 12	Turbulence in Emerging Markets and Impact on Korea	Sung-won Sohn
15-13	Nov 17	Observations on the Korean Economy and North Korea's Economic Potential	Thomas Byrne
15-14	Dec 10	Perspectives on China's Economy and Economic Reform	Huang Haizhou
15-15	Dec 15	Population Aging and Economic Growth in the East Asia and Pacific Region	Sudhir Shetty Philip O'Keefe

2016

No.	Date	Title	Speaker
16-01	Jan 12	The U.S. and Global Prospects and Markets in 2016: A Look Ahead	Allen Sinai
16-02	Feb 23	The Key Themes and Risks of the Global Economy in 2016	Hung Tran
16-03	Mar 2	The U.S. in the Global Economy	Anne Krueger
16-04	May 16	The Prospects and Impact of the U.S. Election and Economy	Martin Feldstein
16-05	May 24	he US and Northeast Asia in a Turbulent Time	Gerald Curtis
16-06	Jun 1	Allies in Business: The Future of the U.S.-ROK Economic Relationship	Mark Lippert
16-07	Sep 20	How Ready Are We for the Fourth Industrial Revolution?	Doh-Yeon Kim
16-08	Oct 21	The World Economy at a Time of Monetary Experimentation and Political Fracture	Charles Dallara
16-09	Nov 10	The U.S. Presidential Election and Its Economic and Security Implications	Marcus Noland & Sung-won Sohn

2017

		Title	Author
17-01	Jan 19	Big Changes, Big Effects - U.S. and Global Economic and Financial Prospects 2017	Allen Sinai
17-02	Mar 13	The 2017 US and Global Macroeconomic Outlook	Martin Feldstein
17-03	Apr 13	Automation, Jobs and the Future of Work in Korea	Jonathan Woetzel
17-04	Jun 8	Trump's US, Japan's Economy and Korea	Gerald Curtis & Hugh Patrick
17-05	Jul 5	Between Brexit and Trump: Global Challenges for the European Union	Thomas Wieser
17-06	Sep 11	Future of Growth	Simon Baptist
17-07	Oct 19	The Future of Work: Is This Time Different?	Carl Benedikt Frey
17-08	Nov 7	The Current State of US Economy and Trump Administration's Trade Policy with Special Reference to the KORUS FTA Revision	Sung-won Sohn & Jeffrey Schott

2018

		Title	Author
18-01	Jan 9	U.S. and Global Prospects Looking Ahead	Allen Sinai
18-02	Mar 13	US Protectionism, China's Political Shift and Their Implications Japan's Labor Reform and Future Korea-Japan Cooperation	Ken Courtis & Yukiko Fukagawa
18-03	Mar 20	Dr. Martin Feldstein's Analysis of the US and Global Economy	Martin Feldstein
18-04	Apr 11	U.S. Economic and Trade Policy for Korea and Asia	Charles Freeman
18-05	Apr 17	How Europeans See China, Changing World Order and Its Implications for Korea	Guy Sorman
18-06	May 15	Asia's New Economic Landscape: India, Japan and China	Eisuke Sakakibara
18-07	Jun 29	Climate, Energy and Green Tech: Transforming Our Economies	Karsten Sach

2019

		Title	Author
19-01	Jan 15	The World in 2019: U.S., Global Economies, Policy and Markets - Can Expansion Be Sustained?	Allen Sinai
19-02	Jan 24	Setting up Canada's National Pension System for Success – CPPIB's Perspective	Suyi Kim
19-03	Feb 19	Why I Remain Optimistic about China: Why China's Worst Enemy in the Short-Term will Prove its Best Friend in the Long-Term	Henny Sender
19-04	Mar 27	Financial Innovation, FinTech and the Future of Finance	Robert Merton
19-05	May 13	5 Ways the Financial System Will Fail Next Time	Michael Barr
19-06	Jun 4	A Brief Tour of Global Near-term Risks and Long-run Concerns about the International Financial Architecture	Carmen Reinhart
19-07	Jun 11	Reflections on the Japanese Economy and Abenomics	Hugh Patrick
19-08	Jul 25	Beyond 1980's: The New Horizon of Japan-Korea Economic Relations	Yukiko Fukagawa
19-09	Sep 27	U.S.-China, Korea-Japan Trade Disputes and the Global Trading System	Jeffrey Schott

		Title	Author
19-10	Oct 22	Financial Innovation and Asset Management Strategies in the Age of Hyper-Low Interest Rates	Robert Merton
19-11	Nov 19	Artificial Intelligence (AI) and its Impact on the Future of Economy and Society	Jerome Glenn

Specialist's Diagnosis

2004

	Title	Author
04-01	A Critical Assessment of Korea's FTA Policy	Chong-hyun Nam
04-02	A Foreign Businessman's Observation on the Korean Economy and Other Things	William C. Oberlin

2005

	Title	Author
05-01	Korea in the World Economy: Challenges and Prospects	Il SaKong

세계경제연구원 간행물

Occasional Paper Series

1993

연번	제목	저자
93-01	Clintonomics and the New World Order: Implications for Korea-US Relations	C. Fred Bergsten
93-02	The Uruguay Round, NAFTA, and US-Korea Economic Relations	Jeffrey Schott

1994

연번	제목	저자
94-01	21세기 준비 어떻게 할 것인가	Paul Kennedy
94-02	미국과 일본 간의 기술경쟁과 한국에 미칠 영향	Ronald A. Morse
94-03	일본경제, 무엇이 문제인가	Toyoo Gyohten
94-04	미국경제와 세계경제: 현황과 전망	Allen Sinai
94-05	국제환율제도 이대로 좋은가	John Williamson
94-06	The Promises of the WTO for the Trading Community	Arthur Dunkel

1995

연번	제목	저자
95-01	멕시코 페소화 위기와 세계금융시장 동향	Charles Dallara
95-02	세계경제 동향과 미국경제 전망	Allen Sinai
95-03	새로운 게임, 새로운 규칙과 새로운 전략	Lester Thurow
95-04	미국·북한관계 전망	Robert Scalapino
95-05	미국의 동아시아 정책과 한반도	James A. Baker III
95-06	미일 무역마찰과 한국	Anne O. Krueger
95-07	동북아경제권 개발 전망: 일본의 시각	Hisao Kanamori

1996

연번	제목	저자
96-01	Trends of International Financial Market and Prospects of Global Economy in 1996	Allen Sinai
96-02	유럽연합(EU)의 앞날과 세계경제	Jørgen Ørstrøm Møller
96-03	세계경제와 OECD의 역할	Donald Johnston
96-04	동아시아 경제성장의 정치적 배경과 영향	Francis Fukuyama

연 번	제 목	저 자
96-05	국제사회에서의 한국의 새 역할	A. W. Clausen

1997

연 번	제 목	저 자
97-01	다국적기업과 동아시아 경제통합	Wendy Dobson
97-02	아태 지역에 대한 미국의 안보정책	William J. Perry
97-03	뉴질랜드의 공공부문 개혁	Donald Hunn

1998

연 번	제 목	저 자
98-01	범세계적 기업과 다자간 투자협정	Edward M. Graham
98-02	변화 속의 안정: 새로운 한미 관계의 모색	W. Anthony Lake
98-03	한국: 동북아의 새로운 협력 중심으로	Donald P. Gregg
98-04	경제적 측면에서 본 독일 통일의 교훈	Juergen B. Donges
98-05	세계화와 종족화: 20세기 말의 딜레마	Guy Sorman

1999

연 번	제 목	저 자
99-01	북한의 정치·경제 상황과 동북아 안보	Marcus Noland
99-02	엔-달러 환율과 국제금융시장	Kenneth S. Courtis
99-03	한국과 아시아 경제: 전망과 정책대응	Donald Johnston/ Hubert Neiss
99-04	미국과 일본경제의 비교평가	Hugh Patrick
99-05	세계경제: 도전과 전망	Rudiger Dornbusch

2000

연 번	제 목	저 자
00-01	한미관계: 번영과 안보의 동반자	Stephen W. Bosworth
00-02	글로벌 뉴 이코노미: 도전과 한국의 활로	양수길
00-03	금융감독의 세계적 조류	이용근
00-04	성장하는 아시아와 침체 속의 일본	Kenneth S. Courtis
00-05	세계금융체제의 미래와 우리의 대응	Morris Goldstein
00-06	시애틀 이후의 WTO와 한미FTA전망	Jeffrey Schott/ 최인범
00-07	다자간 국제경제기구의 미래와 전망	Anne O. Krueger
00-08	남북한 관계: 현황과 전망	Marcus Noland

연 번	제 목	저 자
00-09	Knowledge 시대의 외국인 직접투자 유치	Andrew Fraser
00-10	미국 新행정부 및 의회의 대외·경제정책방향	C. Fred Bergsten
00-11	한미관계: 번영과 안보의 동반자	Stephen W. Bosworth
00-12	2000년 국제금융 및 신흥시장 전망	Charles Dallara/ Robert Hormats
00-13	기업·금융 관계: 현황과 전망	이용근
00-14	금융세계화, 어떻게 대처하나	James P. Rooney

2001

연 번	제 목	저 자
01-01	2001년 미국, 일본경제와 아시아	Kenneth S. Courtis
01-02	부시행정부의 對韓 경제정책과 한국의 대응	Marcus Noland
01-03	3C를 극복하자	Jeffrey D. Jones
01-04	하이테크와 비즈니스, 그리고 세계경제	John Naisbitt
01-05	한국과 IMF	Stanley Fischer
01-06	한국경제의 향후 10년	Dominic Barton
01-07	세계 달러본위제도와 동아시아 환율딜레마	Ronald McKinnon
01-08	新국제질서 속의 유럽과 한국	Pierre Jacquet

2002

연 번	제 목	저 자
02-01	금융위기 再發 어떻게 막나: 칠레의 경험을 중심으로	Carlos Massad
02-02	세계경제의 기회와 위험	Martin Wolf
02-03	美·日 경제현황과 한국의 대응	Marcus Noland
02-04	미국경제와 세계경제: 회복가능성과 위험	Allen Sinai
02-05	세계화: 혜택의 원동력	Patricia Hewitt
02-06	9·11테러사태 이후의 세계질서: 문명의 충돌인가?	Francis Fukuyama
02-07	아시아지역의 통화·금융 협력	Barry Eichengreen
02-08	세계경제, 회복되나?	Kenneth S. Courtis
02-09	미국경제와 달러의 장래	Marcus Noland
02-10	도하라운드: 문제점과 전망	Jagdish Bhagwati
02-11	2003 한국경제와 세계경제 전망	Paul F. Gruenwald
02-12	미국경제 현황과 세계경제의 앞날	John B. Taylor
02-13	9·11사태와 미국의 한반도정책	Thomas C. Hubbard
02-14	미국 경제, 달러 및 대외통상정책 방향	C. Fred Bergsten
02-15	미국의 IT산업 관련 정책과 한국	Peter F. Cowhey

2003

연번	제목	저자
03-01	이라크전 이후의 미국경제와 세계경제	Allen Sinai
03-02	OECD가 본 한국경제	Donald Johnston
03-03	아태 지역에서의 미국의 새 역할	Charles Morrison
03-04	세계경제 전망과 부시행정부의 경기부양책	Phil Gramm
03-05	침체된 독일·유럽 경제가 주는 정책적 교훈과 시사	Hans Tietmeyer
03-06	동아시아 금융협력과 한국	Eisuke Sakakibara
03-07	세계환율체제 개편과 동아시아 경제	John Williamson

2004

연번	제목	저자
04-01	2004 미국경제와 세계경제 전망	Allen Sinai
04-02	김정일 이후의 한반도	Marcus Noland
04-03	미국 대통령 선거와 韓·美·日관계	Hugh Patrick/ Gerald Curtis
04-04	중국경제의 부상과 동북아 지역경제	Zhang Yunling
04-05	아시아 화폐단일화, 가능한가?	Robert Mundell
04-06	외국기업인의 눈에 비친 한국경제	William C. Oberlin

2005

연번	제목	저자
05-01	대통령선거 이후의 미국 통상정책, 어떻게 되나	Peter F. Cowhey
05-02	아시아 경제·무역환경, 어떻게 전개되나?	Dominic Barton
05-03	제2기 부시 행정부의 경제정책과 세계경제 및 시장 전망	Allen Sinai
05-04	일본의 시각에서 본 한국경제의 활로	Yukiko Fukagawa
05-05	세계경제, 무엇이 문제인가	Barry Eichengreen
05-06	세계 속의 한국경제: 역할과 전망	Anne O. Krueger
05-07	중국과 인도가 세계경제에 미치는 영향	Wendy Dobson
05-08	동아시아와 아태지역 경제통합	Robert Scollay
05-09	국제신용평가기관이 보는 한국	Thomas Byrne

2006

연번	제목	저자
06-01	고유가와 세계경제의 앞날	Philip K. Verleger
06-02	2006년 미국경제/세계경제와 금융시장 전망	Allen Sinai

연 번	제 목	저 자
06-03	한미FTA: 지속성장의 활로	Alexander Vershbow
06-04	일본의 대외경제정책과 한일 FTA	Oshima Shotaro
06-05	일본경제 회생과 한국경제	Yukiko Fukagawa
06-06	세계 M&A시장 현황과 전망: 우리의 대응	Robert F. Bruner
06-07	세계인이 보는 한국경제는?	Charles Dallara
06-08	아시아 공통통화와 아시아 경제통합	Eisuke Sakakibara
06-09	미국의 힘은 얼마나 강하며, 중국의 부상은 어떻게 보아야 하는가?	Paul Kennedy/ Bernard Gordon
06-10	- 20년 후의 중국, 어떤 모습일까? - 세계 IT 리더십 경쟁: 승자와 패자	- Richard N. Cooper - George Scalise

2007

연 번	제 목	저 자
07-01	한미관계: 새로운 동반자 시대를 지향하며	Edwin J. Feulner
07-02	통일 이후 독일: 경제침체의 교훈	Juergen B. Donges
07-03	2007년 세계경제와 금융시장의 지각변동	Allen Sinai
07-04	급변하는 세계경제환경, 어떻게 대처해야 하나	Angel Gurría
07-05	동아시아 FTA 가능한가?: 중국의 시각	Zhang Yunling
07-06	구조적 변화 맞고 있는 세계석유시장과 한국	Fereidun Fesharaki
07-07	변모하는 세계경제와 한국	Anne O. Krueger
07-08	되살아나는 일본경제: 전망과 과제	Yukiko Fukagawa
07-09	디지털 네트워크 경제와 글로벌 기업 전략	Ben Verwaayen
07-10	한미FTA: 미국의 시각	Jeffrey Schott
07-11	한미FTA와 한국경제의 미래	Barry Eichengreen
07-12	- 동아시아 경제통합, 어떻게 보나 - 한국경제 및 동아시아경제 전망	- David Hale - Jerald Schiff
07-13	- 21세기는 여전히 미국의 세기가 될 것인가? - 인도경제 전망과 한국 기업	- Guy Sorman - Tarun Das

2008

연 번	제 목	저 자
08-01	국가 미래를 위한 한국의 세계화 전략	Anne O. Krueger
08-02	2008년 미국경제와 세계금융시장 동향	Allen Sinai
08-03	유럽의 경제침체: 우리에게 주는 시사점	Guy Sorman
08-04	차기 미국 대통령이 풀어야할 세계적 도전	James A. Baker III
08-05	일본 자본시장의 현재와 전망	Atsushi Saito

연 번	제 목	저 자
08-06	대선 이후 미국의 정치·경제, 어떻게 전개되나?	Phil Gramm
08-07	세계 및 아시아 경제·금융 전망	Charles Dallara
08-08	한국경제의 경쟁력 강화, 어떻게 하나?	Guy Sorman
08-09	- 국부펀드: 인식과 현실 - 긴장 속의 세계금융시장, 어떻게 되나?	- Robert C. Pozen - Jeffrey R. Shafer

2009

연 번	제 목	저 자
09-01	2009년 한국경제와 세계 및 아시아 경제 전망	Subir Lall
09-02	혼란과 전환기의 경쟁력 강화: 과제와 전망	Deborah Wince-Smith
09-03	위기 속의 미국 및 세계 경제와 금융: 전망과 정책대응	Allen Sinai
09-04	미국 오바마 행정부의 통상정책	Jeffrey Schott
09-05	하강하는 세계경제와 케인지언 정책 처방의 실효성	Justin Yifu Lin
09-06	- 세계금융위기가 개도국에 미치는 여파와 대응 - 최근 세계경제위기의 교훈과 전망	- Danny Leipziger - Anne O. Krueger
09-07	- 미국 오바마 행정부의 경제 및 대외정책, 어떻게 되나? - 한미 경제 파트너십: 세계적 위기에 어떻게 협력할 것인가	- Guy Sorman - Jeffrey Schott

2010

연 번	제 목	저 자
10-01	새로운 세계질서 속에 변화하는 EU: 한국의 기회는?	Jean-Pierre Lehmann
10-02	위기 이후 미국 및 세계경제 전망, 그리고 유산과 정책과제	Allen Sinai
10-03	세계경제, 어떻게 볼 것인가?: 진단과 전망	Anne O. Krueger
10-04	- 세계화 파고 속의 한국과 일본경제: 도전과 전망 - 중국 경제의 虛와 實	- Yukiko Fukagawa - Danny Leipziger
10-05	- 신흥국 자본시장과 뉴 프런티어 - 세계경세와 아시아의 역할	- Mark Mobius - Dominique Strauss-Kahn
10-06	세계경제의 재균형	Paul A. Volcker

2011

연 번	제 목	저 자
11-01	위기 이후의 세계경제와 한국경제: 2011년 및 2012년 전망	Allen Sinai
11-02	원자력 발전의 안전성과 경제성: 한국의 선택은?	장순흥
11-03	중국 경제의 재(再)균형	Yu Yongding
11-04	세계금융질서의 개편: 아시아의 시각	세계경제연구원
11-05	- 아시아 경제의 발전전망과 도전과제 - 유럽의 국가채무위기: 평가와 전망	- Haruhiko Kuroda - Richard N. Cooper
11-06	- 기로에 선 세계화와 다자주의, 그리고 G-20 - 북한의 시장과 경제, 그리고 정치적 안정성, 어떻게 변화하고 있나?	- Danny Leipziger - Marcus Noland

2012

연 번	제 목	저 자
12-01	혼돈 속의 세계경제와 금융시장: 분석과 2012년 전망	Allen Sinai
12-02	- 카이스트의 혁신 - 유로위기 해결책은 없나	- 서남표 - Hans Martens
12-03	- 2012년 미국의 대선과 향후 아태정책 전망 - 세계경제 및 금융시장 현황 - 그래도 세계경제의 미래는 밝다	- Charles Morrison - Charles Dallara - Guy Sorman
12-04	- FTA와 아태지역 통합 그리고 한국 - 유로위기 언제 끝나나?	- Peter A. Petri - Nicolas Véron
12-05	- 중국의 새 리더십과 경제정책 - 국제통상질서의 현황과 WTO의 미래	- Andrew Sheng - Jean-Pierre Lehmann

2013

연 번	제 목	저 자
13-01	2013년 세계경제와 미국경제 전망	Allen Sinai
13-02	유로존, 올해는 위기에서 벗어날 수 있나?	Guntram B. Wolff
13-03	- 유럽국채위기: 과제와 해결책 - 세계경세, 언제 회복되나?	- Andreas Dombret - John Lipsky
13-04	- 미국과 중국경제 현황과 전망 - 일본의 아베노믹스와 외교정책	- David Hale - Hugh Patrick/Gerald Curtis
13-05	- 한국의 창조경제와 문화 - 아베노믹스와 일본 경제의 미래, 그리고 TPP	- Guy Sorman - Yukiko Fukagawa/ Jeffrey Schott
13-06	- 통일 독일의 경제 · 정치적 위상: 한국에 대한 시사점 - 외국인이 바라본 중국의 경제정책	- Karl-Heinz Paqué - Bob Davis

2014

연 번	제 목	저 자
14-01	2014년 세계경제, 나아질 것인가?	Allen Sinai
14-02	- 아베정권은 어디로 가고 있나? - 중견기업: 순항하는 독일경제의 비결	- Gerald Curtis - Peter Friedrich
14-03	- 유럽경제, 살아날 것인가? - 2014년 세계 경제의 향방은?	- Karl-Heinz Paqué - Martin Feldstein
14-04	복지향상과 기부문화	Guy Sorman
14-05	- 세계무역 환경과 세계경제의 미래 - 브릭스(BRICs)에서 미국으로	- Roberto Azevêdo - Sung Won Sohn
14-06	- 세계경제 회복, 위기인가 기회인가 - 아베 정권의 노동개혁과 혁신전략은 성공할 것인가	- Charles Dallara - Yukiko Fukagawa
14-07	- 중국경제 현황과 시진핑의 반부패운동 - 다가올 미 연준의 QE종료가 아시아 금융시장에 미칠 영향 - 중국의 신경제 전략과 한-중 FTA	- Bob Davis - Anoop Singh - Zhang Yunling

2015

연 번	제 목	저 자
15-01	2015년 세계경제, 정상화될 것인가	Allen Sinai
15-02	- 2015년 유럽경제, 회복될 것인가? - 공동 번영을 위한 한미 경제 파트너십 - 독일 하르츠 노동개혁과 한국에 대한 시사점	- Jeroen Dijsselbloem - Mark W. Lippert - Peter Hartz
15-03	- 중국 경제의 앞날을 내다보며 - 유럽의 저성장에서 우리는 무엇을 배워야 하는가?	- Lawrence Lau - Guy Sorman
15-04	- 글로벌 에너지(중점)환경 이슈와 스위스의 경험 - 혼돈의 아시아 경제, 어디로 가는가	- H.E. Doris Leuthard - David L. Asher
15-05	- 중국 경제의 신창타이(新常態)는 무엇인가 - 디지털화를 활용한 독일의 산업혁명 4.0	- Huang Yiping - Matthias Machnig
15-06	- 세상을 바꾸는 네 가지 글로벌 흐름 - 격변하는 신흥시장과 한국에 미칠 영향	- Dominic Barton - Sung-won Sohn
15-07	- 내가 본 한국, 한국 경제, 그리고 북한 경제의 잠재력 - 중국의 경제개혁과 향후 전망	- Thomas Byrne - Huang Haizhou

2016

연 번	제 목	저 자
16-01	2016년 세계경제 및 금융시장 전망	- Allen Sinai
16-02	- 2016년 세계 경제의 주요 이슈와 리스크 - 미국의 경제·정치 상황이 세계 경제에 미치는 영향	- Hung Tran - Anne Krueger
16-03	- 미국 경제와 대선이 세계 경제에 미칠 영향 - 미국 대통령 선거가 동북아에 미칠 지정학적 영향과 전망	- Martin Feldstein - Gerald Curtis

연 번	제 목	저 자
16-04	- 미국 새 행정부의 경제와 안보 정책 - 통화정책 실험과 정치 분열기의 세계 경제 - 한미 경제 협력: 현황과 전망	- Marcus Noland & Sung-won Sohn - Charles Dallara - Mark Lippert

2017

연 번	제 목	저 자
17-01	- 대변혁 속의 2017 - 미국과 세계 경제 금융 전망	- Allen Sinai
17-02	- 미국 신정부의 경제정책과 2017년 미국 및 세계 경제 전망 - 4차 산업혁명 시대 자동화, 일자리, 그리고 직업의 미래	- Martin Feldstein - Jonathan Woetzel
17-03	- 트럼프의 미국, 일본 경제 그리고 한국 - 브렉시트와 미국의 트럼프 대통령: 유럽의 도전	- Gerald Curtis & Hugh Patrick - Thomas Wieser
17-04	- 직업의 미래 - 이번엔 다른가	- Carl Benedikt Frey
17-05	- 세계경제 성장 전망과 기술의 역할 - 미국경제 현황과 트럼프 행정부의 통상정책 및 한미 FTA 개정	- Simon Baptist - Sung-won Sohn &Jeffrey Schott

2018

연 번	제 목	저 자
18-01	- 펠드스타인 교수가 진단하는 미국과 세계경제 - 2018년 미국과 세계 경제·금융 전망	- Martin Feldstein - Allen Sinai
18-02	- 미국 보호주의와 중국 정치체제 변화의 함의 - 일본 노동개혁과 한일 협력의 미래	- Kenneth Courtis - Yukiko Fukagawa
18-03	- 트럼프 행정부의 한국 및 대아시아 무역·경제 정책 - 유럽이 보는 시진핑 체제하의 중국과 세계 질서	- Charles Freeman - Guy Sorman
18-04	- 새로운 아시아 경제 지평: 일본, 중국 그리고 인도 - 독일의 기후변화, 에너지 및 녹색기술 정책 경험과 한국에 대한 시사점	- Eisuke Sakakibara - Karsten Sach

2019

연 번	제 목	저 자
19-01	- 금융혁신, 핀테크 그리고 금융의 미래 - 캐나다 국민연금 시스템의 성공과 CPPIB	- Robert Merton - Suyi Kim
19-02	- 내가 중국 경제를 여전히 낙관하는 이유: 왜 중국의 단기적 악재가 장기적 호재일까 - 2019년 세계 경제 및 금융 전망 - 과연 경기 확장세는 지속될 것인가?	- Henny Sender - Allen Sinai

연 번	제 목	저 자
19-03	국제금융체제의 단기 리스크와 구조적 문제 향후 금융시스템 실패의 5가지 시나리오	-Carmen Reinhart -Michael Barr
19-04	한·일 무역갈등을 넘어서: 양국 경제관계의 새로운 지평 휴 패트릭 교수가 본 일본경제와 아베노믹스	-Yukiko Fukagawa -Hugh Patrick
19-05	초저금리 시대의 금융 혁신과 자산운용 전략	-Robert Merton
19-06	인공지능(AI)이 만드는 경제·사회의 미래 미·중, 한·일 무역분쟁과 세계무역체제	- Jerome Glenn - Jeffrey Schott

보고서 (책자)

연 번	제 목	저 자
94-01	The Global Economy and Korea	사공 일
94-02	탈냉전시대 韓美 정치 · 경제 협력 관계	사공 일/ C. Fred Bergsten
95-01	International Next Generation Leaders' Forum [I]	세계경제연구원
95-02	International Next Generation Leaders' Forum [II]	세계경제연구원
95-03	새로운 韓美 협력체제의 모색	사공 일/ C. Fred Bergsten
96-01	The Multilateral Trading and Financial System	사공 일
96-02	세계화시대의 韓 · 美관계	사공 일/ C. Fred Bergsten
96-03	International Next Generation Leaders' Forum [III]	세계경제연구원
96-04	세계 반도체산업의 발전전망과 한국의 대응전략	세계경제연구원
97-01	Major Issues for the Global Trade and Financial System	사공 일
97-02	한국의 금융개혁	세계경제연구원
98-01	International Next Generation Leaders' Forum [IV]	세계경제연구원
98-02	한반도 통일 및 韓美관계의 현황과 과제	사공 일
98-03	Policy Priorities for the Unified Korean Economy	사공 일/김광석
98-04	The Fifty Years of the GATT/WTO: Past Performance and Future Challenges	사공 일/김광석
99-01	아시아 금융위기의 원인과 대책	사공 일/구영훈
99-02	아시아 금융위기와 한미 관계	세계경제연구원
99-03	For A Better Tomorrow: Asia-Europe Partnership in the 21st Century	ASEM Vision Group
00-01	Reforming the International Financial Architecture: Emerging Market Perspectives	사공 일/왕윤종
00-02	동북아시아포럼 2000	세계경제연구원
00-03	제6차 한미 21세기 위원회 보고서	세계경제연구원
01-01	세계 자유무역 의제를 위한 여건조성	세계경제연구원
01-02	Rebuilding the International Financial Architecture (EMEPG 서울보고서)	Emerging Markets Eminent Persons Group
03-01	새로운 국제질서와 한국의 대응(I) - 새로운 세계질서: 기회와 도전	세계경제연구원
03-01	새로운 국제질서와 한국의 대응(II) - 세계경제 및 주요국 경제의 앞날	세계경제연구원
03-01	새로운 국제질서와 한국의 대응(III) - 한국경제의 진로	세계경제연구원
03-02	세계경제연구원 개원 10주년 국제회의	세계경제연구원

연 번	제 목	저 자
04-01	창업활성화, 어떻게 하나	세계경제연구원
08-01	세계화 시대의 한국 금융산업	세계경제연구원
09-01	최근 세계금융위기, 어떻게 대처할 것인가?	세계경제연구원
10-01	G20 개혁과제: 향후 금융감독 및 규제방향	세계경제연구원
10-02	G20 서울정상회의와 개발의제	세계경제연구원
12-01	새로운 글로벌 금융규제체제: 아시아 금융시장 및 금융기관에 미치는 영향	세계경제연구원
12-02	문화와 한국경제, 그리고 한류	세계경제연구원
12-03	새로운 글로벌 금융시대, 아시아의 미래	세계경제연구원
13-01	중견기업 육성: 독일의 경험에서 배운다	세계경제연구원
13-02	통일과 한국경제	세계경제연구원
13-03	세계 속의 한국 경제 길잡이	세계경제연구원
14-01	리더십과 정책의 우선순위	세계경제연구원
15-01	여성과 성장잠재력	세계경제연구원
17-01	제4차 산업혁명과 한국경제의 미래	세계경제연구원
19-01	디지털 금융시대와 핀테크산업: 부산 금융 중심지의 미래	전광우

IGE Brief+

2012

연번	제목	저자
12-01	문화산업과 서비스교역 그리고 한국경제	남종현
12-02	한일 간 하나의 경제권 형성과 그 추진방향	이종윤
12-03	유럽 경제위기와 한국의 과제	현정택
12-04	이번 대통령 선거, 왜 더욱 중요한가	사공 일
12-05	금융소비자 보호 정책과 금융 옴부즈맨 제도	이재웅
12-06	통일 준비 해둬야	사공 일

2013

연번	제목	저자
13-01	새로운 세계경제 질서와 미래지향적 한일관계	사공 일
13-02	금융개혁과 중국의 정치경제	조윤제

2014

연번	제목	저자
14-01	경찰관이 폭행당해도 놀라지 않는 사회는 미래 없다	사공 일
14-02	경제개혁 3개년 계획 성공하려면	사공 일
14-03	품격 있는 나라를 향한 정부개조	사공 일
14-04	중국의 재부상과 한국: 도전과 기회	사공 일

2016

연번	제목	저자
16-01	세계와 주변 여건은 급변하는데…	사공 일

세계경제지평

1994

연번	제목	저자
94-01	유목적 세계의 도전	Jacques Attali
94-02	세계주의와 지역주의 混在	이영선
94-03	기회와 위험으로서의 中國	김완순
94-04	21세기 준비, 어떻게 할 것인가	Paul Kennedy
94-05	화폐의 종말/자본주의 이후의 사회	홍기택/주한광

연 번	제 목	저 자
94-06	UR 이후 아태 경제협력의 과제와 한국의 선택	유재원
94-07	환경과 무역	나성린/김승진
94-08	円高에 따른 일본의 산업구조 조정과 한국경제의 대응	이종윤
94-09	세계경제환경 변화와 우리의 선택	사공 일
94-10	개방화에 따른 기업정책의 방향	김종석

1995

연 번	제 목	저 자
95-01	한국경제의 위상에 걸맞은 국제적 역할: 도전과 기회	사공 일
95-02	기업의 세계화와 경쟁 규범	김완순
95-03	무엇이 세계화인가	김병주
95-04	한국과 미국: 2000년의 세계경제	James Laney
95-05	세계경제는 좌초할 것인가	김적교
95-06	엔화강세 지속가능성과 우리의 대응	박진근
95-07	세계화와 한국경제: 호황인가 거품인가	구본호
95-08	확산되는 특혜무역협정과 정책과제	남종현
95-09	역사인식과 한일 관계	홍원탁
95-10	일본산업의 네트워크 구조와 그 효율성	이종윤
95-11	국제경쟁력의 갈등	이재웅
95-12	해방 후 우리 경제 반세기의 회고와 전망	김광석

1996

연 번	제 목	저 자
96-01	국내 선물시장의 구상과 전망	이 선
96-02	중소기업시대 열릴 것인가	류동길
96-03	단체교섭제도 有感	배무기
96-04	세계화와 기업의 변신	지 청
96-05	우리나라 금융시장개방의 추진방향	박영철
96-06	다변주의 對 지역주의, 兩立은 가능한가?	김세원
96-07	派生金融商品의 위험과 효용	민상기
96-08	최근 경제위기감의 실체와 대응방향	김광석
96-09	경제발전, 제도개혁, 경쟁질서의 확립	이성섭
96-10	轉機를 맞이한 정부의 기능	김병주
96-11	WTO의 새로운 협상의제	김완순

1997

연 번	제 목	저 자
97-01	노동법개정 難局의 해법: 교섭창구 단일화를 前提한 複數勞組허용	김수곤
97-02	감속성장, 왜 바람직한가	김적교
97-03	韓寶사태의 敎訓	이재웅
97-04	세계화 시대의 경제운영	남덕우
97-05	기업성장의 虛實: 韓寶事態에서 얻는 敎訓	지 청
97-06	북한의 식량난과 집단농장체제	문팔용
97-07	한국의 금융개혁	윤계섭
97-08	高齡化社會의 도래와 財政危機	박종기
97-09	外換危機의 일반모형을 감안한 우리의 대응 방향	박진근
97-10	벤처기업시대를 열어가려면	유동길

1998

연 번	제 목	저 자
98-01	한국의 經濟奇籍은 끝난 것인가?	남종현
98-02	패러다임의 대전환 없이는 위기 극복이 불가능하다	송대희
98-03	기업구조조정과 바람직한 은행-기업관계	남상우
98-04	새로운 기업지배구조의 모색과 사외이사의 역할	이영기
98-05	고투자-고저축 고리의 단절을 위한 제언	이영탁

1999

연 번	제 목	저 자
99-01	연금개혁의 전망과 과제	박종기
99-02	지하철파업과 다시 보는 노조전임자 문제	김수곤
99-03	금융구조조정과 중소기업금융	박준경
99-04	21세기를 향한 환경정책과제	김종기
99-05	소득분배 문제의 실상과 대응방향	김광석
99-06	"생산적 복지" 정책의 허와 실	최 광
99-07	세계화시대의 韓中日 經濟協力 强化 方案	사공 일
99-08	시애틀 WTO 각료회의의 결렬과 향후전망	박태호

2000

연 번	제 목	저 자
00-01	2000년 경제전망 및 향후 과제	김준경
00-02	세계금융체제에 관한 논의, 어떻게 되고 있나	사공 일

연 번	제 목	저 자
00-03	아시아 금융위기와 한국경제의 미래	사공 일
00-04	高비용 低능률구조의 부활	이종윤
00-05	아시아 경제회복, 지속될 것인가?	사공 일
00-06	국제경제환경과 한국경제	조윤제
00-07	기업경영 감시를 위한 기관투자가의 역할	이재웅
00-08	미국의 구조조정 경험과 교훈	이영세

2001

연 번	제 목	저 자
01-01	한국산업의 경쟁력 위기와 향후 진로	김도훈
01-02	주 5일 근무제 도입 신중해야	박영범

연구보고서 (세계경제 시리즈)

1994

연 번	제 목	저 자
94-01	UR이후 아태 경제협력의 과제와 한국의 선택	유재원
94-02	환경-무역관계가 한국 무역에 미치는 영향	김승진/나성린
94-03	円高에 따른 일본의 산업구조조정과 한국경제의 대응	이종윤
94-04	개방화에 따른 기업정책의 방향	김종석

1995

연 번	제 목	저 자
95-01	국내 외국인직접투자 현황과 정책대응	주한광/김승진
95-02	비즈니스 리엔지니어링 기업: 한·일 기업의 수용 가능성 비교	이재규
95-03	WTO 체제와 우리의 대응	김지홍

1996

연 번	제 목	저 자
96-01	국내 선물시장에 대한 구상과 전망	이 신
96-02	일본 산업의 네트워크구조와 그 효율성	이종윤

1997

연 번	제 목	저 자
97-01	루마니아의 경제현황과 주요개혁과제	김광석/김병주/고일동

1998

연 번	제 목	저 자
98-01	우리 경제의 成長要因과 成長潛在力 展望	김광석
98-02	한국과 ASEAN 諸國 間 무역구조의 변화 추이와 대응방향	김승진
98-03	국제무역체계의 도전과제	김완순/최낙균
98-04	정보화의 세계적 추세와 우리의 대응방안	박종국

2000

연 번	제 목	저 자
00-01	한국의 금융 위기와 산업 정책	이영세/정용승

2001

연 번	제 목	저 자
01-01	우리나라의 산업·무역 정책 전개 과정	김광석
01-02	한국에서의 기술이전과 정보의 역할	이영세

전문가 진단

2004

연 번	제 목	저 자
04-01	한국 FTA정책의 虛와 實	남종현
04-02	외국 기업인의 눈에 비친 한국경제	William C. Oberlin

2005

연 번	제 목	저 자
05-01	세계 속의 한국경제: 과제와 전망	사공 일

세계경제연구원 특별강연

1993

연 번	제 목	연 사
93-01	클린턴 행정부의 경제정책과 한미 경제관계	C. Fred Bergsten
93-02	UR 및 NAFTA의 장래와 한국의 대응	Jeffrey Schott
93-03	국제환경 변화와 세계경제 장·단기 전망	Allen Sinai
93-04	태평양지역 경제전망과 한국의 대응	Lawrence Krauss
93-05	21세기 세계구도 변화와 한국	Jacques Attali

1994

연 번	제 목	연 사
94-01	21세기 준비 어떻게 할 것인가?	Paul Kennedy
94-02	미국과 일본 간의 기술경쟁과 한국에 미칠 영향	Ronald A. Morse
94-03	일본경제 무엇이 문제인가?	Toyoo Gyohten
94-04	미국경제와 세계경제 현황과 전망	Allen Sinai
94-05	동구권 경제전망과 한국의 진출방안	Ronald Freeman
94-06	국제환율제도 이대로 좋은가?	John Williamson
94-07	새로운 국제무역질서와 한국의 대응	Arthur Dunkel
94-08	新경제의 금융개혁: 평가와 전망	박재윤

1995

연 번	제 목	연 사
95-01	세계화 전략과 앞으로의 경제운용방향	홍재형
95-02	멕시코 페소화 위기와 세계 금융시장 동향	Charles Dallara
95-03	세계경제 동향과 미국경제 전망	Allen Sinai
95-04	한국과 미국: 2000년의 세계경제	James Laney
95-05	새로운 게임, 새로운 규칙과 새로운 전략	Lester Thurow
95-06	미국-북한 관계 전망	Robert Scalapino
95-07	미국의 동아시아 정책과 한반도	James A. Baker Ⅲ
95-08	미일 무역마찰과 한국	Anne O. Krueger
95-09	국제금융제도 무엇이 문제인가?	Stanley Fischer
95-10	세계무역기구 - 새로운 도전	Jagdish Bhagwati
95-11	동북아 경제권 개발 전망	Kanamori Hisao
95-12	러시아 정보제도의 현황과 변화 전망	Vadim Kirpitchenko
95-13	최근의 국제금융시장 동향과 96년도 세계경제 전망	Allen Sinai
95-14	최근 미국 정치동향과 한미 관계	Thomas Foley

연번	제목	연사
95-15	APEC과 세계무역체제	C. Fred Bergsten
95-16	국제금융제도의 현황과 향후 전망	Toyoo Gyohten
95-17	WTO와 세계무역체제	Anne O. Krueger

1996

연번	제목	연사
96-01	세계경제의 도전과 한국	Robert Lawrence
96-02	新경제의 통상정책	박재윤
96-03	다자간 무역체제 하의 기술협약과 한국	Sylvia Ostry
96-04	정보화 시대: 한국의 대응	이석채
96-05	EU의 앞날과 세계경제	Jørgen Ørstrøm Møller
96-06	세계경제와 OECD의 역할	Donald Johnston
96-07	다자간 무역체제 하의 새로운 과제	김철수
96-08	금융세계화와 세계경제	Paul A. Volcker
96-09	세계경제와 동아시아경제: 협력인가, 갈등인가?	Martin Wolf
96-10	다국적 기업의 세계화 전략과 동아시아 경제통합	Wendy Dobson
96-11	위기에 처한 일본의 은행부문: 원인과 시사점	Hugh Patrick
96-12	동아시아 경제성장의 정치적 배경과 영향	Francis Fukuyama
96-13	클린턴 행정부의 업적과 재선 전망 및 한국에 미칠 영향	Robert Warne
96-14	세계무역 – 21세기 비전	C. Fred Bergsten
96-15	국제사회에서의 한국의 새 역할	A. W. Clausen
96-16	제2기 클린턴 행정부의 통상정책	Richard Feinberg

1997

연번	제목	연사
97-01	세계화 시대의 경제운용	남덕우
97-02	경제적 측면에서 본 통독의 교훈	Juergen B. Donges
97-03	아태 지역에 대한 미국의 안보정책	William Perry
97-04	범세계적 기업과 다자간 투자협정	Edward Graham
97-05	뉴질랜드의 공공부문 개혁	Donald Hunn
97-06	한미 관계: 변화 속의 안정	W. Anthony Lake
97-07	한국: 동북아의 새로운 협력 중심으로	Donald P. Gregg
97-08	일본의 경제침체와 동아시아 통화위기	Ronald McKinnon

1998

연 번	제 목	연 사
98-01	세계화와 국가의 주체성	Guy Sorman
98-02	아시아 통화위기와 일본의 역할	Takatoshi Kato
98-03	한국의 통화·금융위기: 미국의 시각	Charles Dallara
98-04	유럽 단일통화(Euro)와 세계금융 질서	Tue Rohsted
98-05	아시아 통화위기: 원인과 전망	Anne O. Krueger
98-06	국가경영혁신, 어떻게 할 것인가?	진 념
98-07	99년의 아시아와 한국경제 전망	Hubert Neiss
98-08	최근 북한 경제상황과 향후 전망	Marcus Noland

1999

연 번	제 목	연 사
99-01	세계 속의 한국경제와 OECD	Donald Johnston
99-02	미국의 경제현황과 주식시장 전망	Richard A. Grasso
99-03	국제금융시장과 달러/엔 환율 전망	Kenneth S. Courtis
99-04	미국과 일본 경제의 비교평가	Hugh Patrick
99-05	세계경제: 도전과 전망	Rudiger Dornbusch
99-06	한국의 금융세계화, 어떻게 해야 하나?	James P. Rooney
99-07	국제금융시장 전망: 미국경제와 금융시장을 중심으로	Robert Hormats
99-08	한미관계: 번영과 안보의 동반자	Stephen W. Bosworth

2000

연 번	제 목	연 사
00-01	2000년도 아시아 및 신흥시장 전망	Charles Dallara
00-02	글로벌 뉴 이코노미: 도전과 한국의 활로	양수길
00-03	성장하는 아시아와 침체 속의 일본	Kenneth S. Courtis
00-04	세계금융체제의 미래와 우리의 대응	Morris Goldstein
00-05	기업·금융 구조조정의 향후 정책방향	이용근
00-06	시애틀 이후 WTO와 한미FTA 전망	Jeffrey Schott
00-07	세계경제체제 변화: 전망과 정책대응	Anne O. Krueger
00-08	남북한 관계: 현황과 전망	Marcus Noland
00-09	지식시대의 외국인 직접투자 유치	Andrew Fraser
00-10	미국 新행정부 및 의회의 경제·대외 정책방향	C. Fred Bergsten

2001

연번	제목	연사
01-01	2001년 미국, 일본 경제와 아시아	Kenneth S. Courtis
01-02	부시행정부의 對韓정책과 한국의 대응	Marcus Noland
01-03	내가 본 한국기업과 한국경제: 3C를 극복하자	Jeffrey D. Jones
01-04	하이테크와 비즈니스, 그리고 세계경제	John Naisbitt
01-05	한국과 IMF	Stanley Fischer
01-06	한국경제의 향후 10년	Dominic Barton
01-07	세계 달러본위제도와 동아시아 환율딜레마	Ronald McKinnon
01-08	新국제질서 속의 유럽과 한국	Pierre Jacquet
01-09	세계경제의 기회와 위험: 긴급진단	Martin Wolf
01-10	금융위기 再發, 어떻게 막나: 칠레의 경험을 중심으로	Carlos Massad
01-11	21세기 미일 경제관계 전망과 한국의 대응과제	Marcus Noland

2002

연번	제목	연사
02-01	세계화: 혜택의 원동력	Patricia Hewitt
02-02	9·11 테러사태 이후의 세계질서: 문명의 충돌인가?	Francis Fukuyama
02-03	아시아 지역의 통화·금융 협력	Barry Eichengreen
02-04	미국경제와 세계경제: 회복가능성과 위험	Allen Sinai
02-05	세계경제, 회복되고 있나?	Kenneth S. Courtis
02-06	미국경제와 달러의 장래	Marcus Noland
02-07	도하라운드: 문제점과 전망	Jagdish Bhagwati
02-08	2003년 한국경제와 세계경제	Paul F. Gruenwald
02-09	미국경제, 달러 및 대외통상 정책 방향	C. Fred Bergsten
02-10	9·11 사태 1주년과 미국의 한반도 정책	Thomas C. Hubbard
02-11	미국경제 현황과 세계경제의 앞날	John B. Taylor
02-12	미국의 IT산업 관련정책과 한국	Peter F. Cowhey

2003

연번	제목	연사
03-01	이라크전 이후의 미국경제와 세계경제	Allen Sinai
03-02	2003 세계경제와 한국: OECD의 시각	Donald Johnston
03-03	亞太지역에서의 미국의 새 역할	Charles Morrison
03-04	세계경제 전망과 부시행정부의 경기부양책	Phil Gramm
03-05	세계환율체제 개편과 동아시아 경제	John Williamson
03-06	침체된 독일·유럽경제가 주는 교훈과 정책적 시사	Hans Tietmeyer

연번	제목	연사
03-07	동아시아 금융협력과 한국	Eisuke Sakakibara

2004

연번	제목	연사
04-01	2004년 미국경제와 세계경제 전망	Allen Sinai
04-02	김정일 이후의 한반도	Marcus Noland
04-03	외국기업인의 눈에 비친 한국경제	William C. Oberlin
04-04	미국 대통령선거와 韓美日 관계 - 미국 대통령선거와 韓美, 韓日 관계 - 미국 경제와 일본경제, 그리고 한국경제	- Gerald Curtis - Hugh Patrick
04-05	중국경제의 부상과 동북아 지역경제	Zhang Yunling
04-06	아시아 화폐 단일화, 가능한가?	Robert Mundell
04-07	대통령선거 이후의 미국 통상정책, 어떻게 되나	Peter F. Cowhey
04-08	아시아 세계무역환경, 어떻게 전개되나?	Dominic Barton

2005

연번	제목	연사
05-01	제2기 부시행정부의 경제정책과 세계경제 및 시장 전망	Allen Sinai
05-02	일본의 시각에서 본 한국경제의 활로	Yukiko Fukagawa
05-03	국제신용평가기관이 보는 한국	Thomas Byrne
05-04	급부상하는 중국과 인도 경제	Wendy Dobson
05-05	동아시아와 아태지역 경제통합	Robert Scollay
05-06	세계 속의 한국경제: 역할과 전망	Anne O. Krueger
05-07	세계경제, 무엇이 문제인가	Barry Eichengreen
05-08	미국의 힘은 얼마나 강한가?	Paul Kennedy
05-09	중국의 부상, 어떻게 보아야 하나	Bernard Gordon
05-10	고유가와 세계경제의 앞날	Philip K. Verleger

2006

연번	제목	연사
06-01	2006년 미국경제/세계경제와 금융시장 전망	Allen Sinai
06-02	한미FTA: 지속성장의 활로	Alexander Vershbow
06-03	일본 경제회생과 한국경제	Yukiko Fukagawa
06-04	세계 IT 리더십 경쟁: 승자와 패자	George Scalise
06-05	세계인이 보는 한국경제는?	Charles Dallara
06-06	일본의 대외경제정책과 한일 FTA	Oshima Shotaro

연번	제목	연사
06-07	20년 후의 중국, 어떻게 될까?	Richard N. Cooper
06-08	세계 M&A 시장 현황과 전망: 우리의 대응	Robert F. Bruner
06-09	한미 관계: 새로운 동반자 시대를 지향하며	Edwin J. Feulner
06-10	아시아 공동통화와 아시아 경제통합	Eisuke Sakakibara
06-11	통일 이후 독일: 경제침체의 교훈	Juergen B. Donges
06-12	급변하는 세계경제환경, 어떻게 대처해야 하나?	Angel Gurría
06-13	동아시아 FTA, 가능한가?: 중국의 시각	Zhang Yunling
06-14	구조적 변화 맞고 있는 세계석유시장과 한국	Fereidun Fesharaki
06-15	변모하는 세계경제와 한국	Anne O. Krueger

2007

연번	제목	연사
07-01	2007년 세계경제와 금융시장의 지각변동	Allen Sinai
07-02	되살아나는 일본경제: 전망과 과제	Yukiko Fukagawa
07-03	디지털 네트워크 경제와 글로벌 기업전략	Ben Verwaayen
07-04	동아시아 경제, 어디로 갈 것인가?	David Hale
07-05	2008년 미국 대통령선거, 어떻게 될 것인가?	Stephen J. Yates
07-06	세계 속의 한국경제, 위상강화 어떻게 하나?	Charles Dallara
07-07	한미FTA: 미국의 시각	Jeffrey Schott
07-08	한미FTA와 한국경제의 미래	Barry Eichengreen
07-09	왜 21세기에도 미국의 세기가 될 것인가?	Guy Sorman
07-10	인도경제 전망과 한국기업	Tarun Das
07-11	세계화시대의 기업 인재 확보	Ben Verwaayen
07-12	2008년 한국경제와 동아시아 경제 전망	Jerald Schiff
07-13	국가 미래를 위한 한국의 세계화 전략	Anne O. Krueger

2008

연번	제목	연사
08-01	2008년 미국경제와 세계금융시장 전망	Allen Sinai
08-02	국부펀드(Sovereign Wealth Funds): 인식과 현실	Robert C. Pozen
08-03	유럽의 경제침체: 우리에게 주는 시사점	Guy Sorman
08-04	차기 미국대통령이 풀어야 할 세계적 도전	James A. Baker Ⅲ
08-05	일본 자본시장의 현재와 전망	Atsushi Saito
08-06	대선 이후 미국의 정치·경제, 어떻게 전개되나?	Phil Gramm
08-07	세계 및 아시아 경제·금융, 어떻게 되나?	Charles Dallara

연 번	제 목	연 사
08-08	한국경제의 경쟁력 강화, 어떻게 하나?	Guy Sorman
08-09	긴장 속의 세계금융시장, 어떻게 되나?	Jeffrey Shafer
08-10	세계금융위기, 달러, 그리고 유가	Martin Feldstein
08-11	09년 한국경제와 세계 및 아시아경제 전망	Subir Lall

2009

연 번	제 목	연 사
09-01	혼란과 전환기의 경쟁력 강화: 과제와 전망	Deborah Wince-Smith
09-02	위기 속의 미국 및 세계경제와 금융: 전망과 정책대응	Allen Sinai
09-03	세계금융위기가 개도국에 미치는 여파와 우리의 대응	Danny Leipziger
09-04	미국 오바마 행정부의 통상정책	Jeffrey Schott
09-05	미국 오바마 행정부의 경제 및 대외정책, 어떻게 되나?	Guy Sorman
09-06	최근 세계경제위기와 우리의 교훈	Anne O. Krueger
09-07	하강하는 세계경제와 케인지언 정책처방의 실효성	Justin Yifu Lin
09-08	최근 세계경제위기와 한미 협력관계: 과제와 전망	Jeffrey Schott
09-09	경제위기 이후 세계의 투자 전망: IFC와 개도국의 역할	Lars H. Thunell
09-10	과연 더블딥 경제침체는 올 것인가?	손성원
09-11	새로운 세계 질서 속에서 변화하는 EU: 한국의 기회는?	Jean-Pierre Lehmann

2010

연 번	제 목	연 사
10-01	위기 이후의 미국 및 세계경제 전망, 그리고 유산과 정책과제	Allen Sinai
10-02	세계화 파고 속의 한국과 일본경제: 도전과 전망	Yukiko Fukagawa
10-03	신흥국 자본시장과 뉴 프론티어	Mark Mobius
10-04	중국 경제의 虛와 實: 과제와 전망	Danny Leipziger
10-05	세계경제와 아시아의 역할	Dominique Strauss-Kahn
10-06	세계경제, 어떻게 볼 것인가?: 진단과 전망	Anne O. Krueger
10-07	더블딥과 디플레이션의 가능성은 얼마나 될까?	손성원
10-08	세계경제의 재균형	Paul A. Volcker

2011

연 번	제 목	연 사
11-01	위기 이후의 세계경제와 한국경제: 2011년 및 2012년 전망	Allen Sinai
11-02	아시아 경제의 발전전망과 도전과제	Haruhiko Kuroda

연 번	제 목	연 사
11-03	유럽국가의 채무위기: 평가와 전망	Richard N. Cooper
11-04	원자력발전의 안전성과 경제성: 한국의 선택은?	장순흥
11-05	기로에 선 세계화와 다자주의, 그리고 G20	Danny Leipziger
11-06	북한의 시장과 경제, 그리고 정치적 안정성, 어떻게 변화하고 있나?	Marcus Noland
11-07	중국경제 재균형에 관한 특강	Yu Yongding
11-08	격동 속의 세계경제: 전망과 투자전략	손성원

2012

연 번	제 목	연 사
12-01	혼돈 속의 미국경제와 세계경제 그리고 금융시장, 어떻게 되나?	Allen Sinai
12-02	12년 미국의 대선과 향후 아태 정책 전망	Charles Morrison
12-03	과학기술 연구대학의 발전과 교육, 경제성장	서남표
12-04	유로 위기: 해결책은 없나?	Hans Martens
12-05	세계경제 및 금융시장 현황	Charles Dallara
12-06	그래도 세계경제의 미래는 밝다	Guy Sorman
12-07	FTA와 아태지역통합, 그리고 한국	Peter A. Petri
12-08	유로 위기: 언제 끝나나?	Nicolas Véron
12-09	중국의 새 리더십과 경제정책	Andrew Sheng
12-10	국제통상질서의 현황과 WTO의 미래	Jean-Pierre Lehmann

2013

연 번	제 목	연 사
13-01	2013년 세계경제와 미국경제 전망	Allen Sinai
13-02	유로존, 올해는 위기에서 벗어날 수 있나?	Guntram B. Wolff
13-03	유럽국채위기: 과제와 해결책	Andreas Dombret
13-04	세계경제, 언제 회복되나?	John Lipsky
13-05	미국과 중국경제 현황과 전망	David Hale
13-06	일본의 아베노믹스와 외교정책	Hugh Patrick, Gerald Curtis
13-07	한국의 창조경제와 문화	Guy Sorman
13-08	아베노믹스와 일본경제의 미래, 그리고 TPP	Yukiko Fukagawa, Jeffrey Schott
13-09	통일 독일의 경제·정치적 위상: 한국에 대한 시사점	Karl-Heinz Paqué
13-10	외국인이 바라본 중국의 경제정책	Bob Davis

연 번	제 목	연 사
13-11	일본 아베정권의 정치·경제정책이 우리에게 미칠 영향은?	David Asher
13-12	한중일 정치·경제 관계 어디로 가고 있나?	David Philling

2014

연 번	제 목	연 사
14-01	2014년 세계경제, 나아질 것인가	Allen Sinai
14-02	스위스 메이드	R. James Breiding
14-03	아베정권은 어디로 가고 있나	Gerald Curtis
14-04	중견기업: 순항하는 독일 경제의 비결	Peter Friedrich
14-05	유럽경제, 살아날 것인가?	Karl-Heinz Paqué
14-06	2014년 세계경제의 향방은?	Martin Feldstein
14-07	복지향상과 기부문화	Guy Sorman
14-08	세계무역 환경 변화와 세계경제의 미래	Roberto Azevêdo
14-09	브릭스(BRICs)에서 미국으로	Sung Won Sohn
14-10	세계경제 회복, 위기인가 기회인가	Charles Dallara
14-11	아베의 노동개혁과 혁신전략은 성공할 것인가	Yukiko Fukagawa
14-12	중국경제 현황과 시진핑의 반부패운동	Bob Davis
14-13	다가올 미 연준의 QE 종료가 아시아 금융시장에 미칠 영향	Anoop Singh
14-14	중국의 신경제전략과 한중 FTA	Zhang Yunling

2015

연 번	제 목	연 사
15-01	2015년 유럽경제, 회복될 것인가	Jeroen Dijsselbloem
15-02	2015년 세계경제, 정상화될 것인가	Allen Sinai
15-03	중국 경제의 앞날을 내다보며	Lawrence Lau
15-04	공동 번영을 위한 한미 경세 파트너십	Mark W. Lippert
15-05	독일 하르츠 노동개혁과 한국에 대한 시사점	Peter Hartz
15-06	유럽의 저성장에서 우리는 무엇을 배워야 하는가?	Guy Sorman
15-07	글로벌 에너지·환경 이슈와 스위스의 경험	Doris Leuthard
15-08	혼돈의 아시아 경제, 어디로 가는가	David L. Asher
15-09	중국 경제의 신창타이(新常態)는 무엇인가	Huang Yiping
15-10	디지털화를 활용한 독일의 산업혁명 4.0	Matthias Machnig
15-11	세상을 바꾸는 네 가지 글로벌 흐름	Dominic Barton
15-12	격변하는 신흥시장과 한국에 미칠 영향	Sung-won Sohn

연 번	제 목	연 사
15-13	내가 본 한국, 한국 경제, 그리고 북한 경제의 잠재력	Thomas Byrne
15-14	중국의 경제개혁과 향후 전망	Huang Haizhou
15-15	동아태지역 국가의 인구 노령화 문제와 경제성장 전망	Sudhir Shetty Philip O'Keefe

2016

연 번	제 목	연 사
16-01	2016년 세계경제 및 금융시장 전망	Allen Sinai
16-02	2016년 세계 경제의 주요 이슈와 리스크	Hung Tran
16-03	미국의 경제·정치 상황이 세계 경제에 미치는 영향	Anne Krueger
16-04	미국 경제와 대선이 세계 경제에 미칠 영향	Martin Feldstein
16-05	미국 대통령 선거가 동북아에 미칠 지정학적 영향과 전망	Gerald Curtis
16-06	한미 경제 협력: 현황과 전망	Mark Lippert
16-07	제4차 산업혁명, 우리의 준비는	Doh-Yeon Kim
16-08	통화정책 실험과 정치 분열기의 세계 경제	Charles Dallara
16-09	미국 새 행정부의 경제와 안보 정책	Marcus Noland & Sung-won Sohn

2017

연 번	제 목	연 사
17-01	대변혁 속의 2017 – 미국과 세계 경제 금융 전망	Allen Sinai
17-02	미국 신정부의 경제정책과 2017년 미국 및 세계 경제 전망	Martin Feldstein
17-03	4차 산업혁명 시대 자동화, 일자리, 그리고 직업의 미래	Jonathan Woetzel
17-04	트럼프의 미국, 일본 경제 그리고 한국	Gerald Curtis & Hugh Patrick
17-05	브렉시트와 미국의 트럼프 대통령: 유럽의 도전	Thomas Wieser
17-06	세계경제 성장 전망과 기술의 역할	Simon Baptist
17 07	직업의 미래 – 이번엔 나른가	Carl Benedikt Frey
17-08	미국경제 현황과 트럼프 행정부의 통상정책 및 한미FTA 개정	Sung-won Sohn & Jeffrey Schott

2018

연 번	제 목	연 사
18-01	2018년 미국과 세계 경제·금융 전망	Allen Sinai
18-02	미국 보호주의와 중국 정치체제 변화의 함의 일본 노동개혁과 한일 협력의 미래	Ken Courtis & Yukiko Fukagawa

연 번	제 목	연 사
18-03	펠드스타인 교수가 진단하는 미국과 세계경제	Martin Feldstein
18-04	트럼프 행정부의 한국 및 대아시아 무역·경제 정책	Charles Freeman
18-05	유럽이 보는 시진핑 체제하의 중국과 세계 질서	Guy Sorman
18-06	새로운 아시아 경제 지평: 일본, 중국 그리고 인도	Eisuke Sakakibara
18-07	독일의 기후변화, 에너지 및 녹색기술 정책 경험과 한국에 대한 시사점	Karsten Sach

2019

연 번	제 목	연 사
19-01	2019년 세계 경제 및 금융 전망: 과연 경기 확장세는 지속될 것인가	Allen Sinai
19-02	캐나다 국민연금 시스템의 성공과 CPPIB	Suyi Kim
19-03	내가 중국 경제를 여전히 낙관하는 이유: 왜 중국의 단기적 악재가 장기적 호재일까	Henny Sender
19-04	금융혁신, 핀테크 그리고 금융의 미래	Robert Merton
19-05	향후 금융 시스템 실패의 5가지 시나리오	Michael Barr
19-06	국제금융체제의 단기 리스크와 구조적 문제	Carmen Reinhart
19-07	휴 패트릭 교수가 본 일본경제와 아베노믹스	Hugh Patrick
19-08	한·일 무역갈등을 넘어서: 양국 경제관계의 새로운 지평	Yukiko Fukagawa
19-09	미·중, 한·일 무역분쟁과 세계무역체제	Jeffrey Schott
19-10	초저금리 시대의 금융 혁신과 자산운용 전략	Robert Merton
19-11	인공지능(AI)이 만드는 경제·사회의 미래	Jerome Glenn